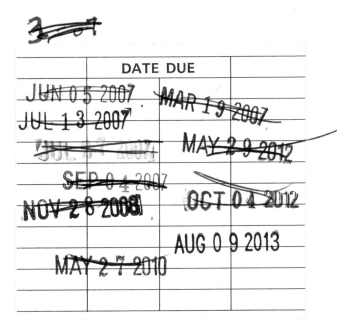

THE ELEMENTS OF GREAT PUBLIC SPEAKING

THE ELEMENTS OF GREAT PUBLIC SPEAKING

HOW TO BE
CALM, CONFIDENT, AND COMPELLING

J. Lyman MacInnis

TEN SPEED PRESS
Berkeley | Toronto

Copyright © 2006 by J. Lyman MacInnis

Ten Speed Press
PO Box 7123
Berkeley, California 94707
www.tenspeed.com

Distributed in Australia by Simon and Schuster Australia, in Canada by Ten Speed Press Canada, in New Zealand by Southern Publishers Group, in South Africa by Real Books, and in the United Kingdom and Europe by Publishers Group UK.

Cover and text design by Betsy Stromberg

Library of Congress Cataloging-in-Publication Data

MacInnis, J. Lyman.
  The elements of great public speaking : how to be calm, confident, and compelling / J. Lyman MacInnis.
      p. cm.
  Includes index.
  ISBN-13: 978-1-58008-780-3
  ISBN-10: 1-58008-780-9
  1. Public speaking. 2. Public speaking--Psychological aspects. I. Title.
  PN4129.15.M34 2006
  808.5'1--dc22

                              2006015250

Printed in the United States
First printing, 2006
1 2 3 4 5 6 7 8 9 10 – 10 09 08 07 06

This book is dedicated to Liam, Will, and Spencer MacInnis, who are just beginning life's great journey.

CONTENTS

Thanks

Special thanks to my wife, Anne, and our sons and daughters-in-law, Matthew, Beverley, Alan, and Anna, for their reviews and comments; to John Vaillancourt and David Matheson, for their helpful suggestions; and to Don MacAdam, a great friend and finely tuned sounding board. Thanks, too, to Ten Speed's Clancy Drake and copy editor Holly Taines White for all their improvements.

TALK ISN'T CHEAP

The adage says that talk is cheap. Well, it isn't. Talk can be extremely expensive, both literally and figuratively.

The next time you attend a business presentation, make a guess at how much in salary it costs to have all those people attend. Now factor in the probable salary cost of preparation; it would have to be at least a few thousand dollars. Add to that the actual out-of-pocket expenses of preparing and putting on the presentation. Then consider what the *lost* cost is if the presentation is not as effective as it could be, or worse, if it fails completely. Taking the time to properly plan for and deliver a presentation may make or save your organization more money in an hour than is achieved in a year of routine work. Superior communications lead to such increased profitability that it's impossible to put an accurate dollar value on them.

Sit through twenty business presentations and you will find them almost indistinguishable. Business presentations tend to be too long, poorly delivered, and completely forgettable. This is usually because the people designing and presenting them aren't sufficiently trained in the skills required to properly prepare and deliver an effective and persuasive talk.

And it isn't just for corporations and professional organizations that talk isn't cheap. Competent, well-educated, talented people often find their earning capacity limited because they can't effectively communicate their ideas, particularly when standing in front of a group. How well you communicate determines whether you're memorable or forgettable, boring or interesting, and whether people will ignore you or listen to you. Poor eye contact and mumbling have been known to sidetrack careers. The inability to organize and clearly articulate their thoughts has prevented people from all walks of life from achieving their goals and reaching their potential.

People are attracted to articulate, well-organized, forceful speakers. If you communicate well you will do well. But if you communicate best (meaning that you look, sound, and act like someone who is worth listening to and following) you will flourish.

Business leaders and professionals can no longer maintain low profiles. They now have to function effectively in an omnipresent communications environment that used to be restricted to celebrities and politicians. Today's business leaders are wide open to public scrutiny and, like politicians have had to for decades, need to gain the support of a number of constituencies, including peers, employees, clients, suppliers, shareholders, regulators, consumer activists, and occasionally the most important of all, the media. A successful business leader must have the ability to relate to people both within and outside his or her organization.

Concerned citizens wishing to make a difference in their communities need to develop the same speaking skills as do people in business. Taking the time to properly prepare and deliver an effective talk may result in persuading your local council to install those traffic lights that could save lives. Or you might successfully raise the funds to build a much-needed playground. Perhaps you simply want to do a good job of welcoming your new daughter-in-law into your family, or, as president of the PTA, pay a nice tribute to a respected teacher who's retiring. Whatever your purpose, a properly prepared and effectively delivered talk will considerably increase your chances of success and at the same time enhance your reputation as a leader.

You can't be a real leader if you don't have the power of persuasion. There's little point in knowing how to solve a problem if you can't communicate the solution in a way that will encourage people to act. You must be able to organize your thoughts to convincingly present your case. If you can't communicate effectively, you will have great difficulty making things happen, and you certainly won't be able to make them happen the way you want them to or when you want them to.

Whether you're the CEO of a Fortune 500 company, an upcoming professional in a thriving practice, a struggling young entrepreneur, or that person who simply wants to make a difference, you will find that one of the most rewarding experiences in life is standing in front of a group of people and bringing them around to your point of view. Every speaking opportunity is a chance to influence one person, some people, or perhaps thousands. Perception really is reality. If an audience, whether of one or hundreds, doesn't perceive the speaker to be an effective person, then that speaker is going to fail in his or her main purpose, whether that is to inform, persuade, motivate, or entertain. Effective speakers will become today's leadership elite.

To be an effective speaker you first have to know what you're talking about. You must have sufficiently prepared yourself, through experience or study (preferably both), to talk about a particular subject. You also have to care about your topic, and you have to want to convey your message to others.

Then you need to understand everything you possibly can about your audience, whatever its size. Next, you have to craft your message in your listeners' terms. To persuade an audience to your point of view you have to clearly show them what's in it for them, not what's in it for you; to do this you have to present your message in a way that they can easily understand and relate to. Finally, you have to develop a winning style, encompassing what you do and how you do it, what you say and how you say it.

Few of us are born with the necessary skills to achieve all of this, but, like playing a musical instrument, swimming, or riding a bicycle, these skills can be acquired and developed through study, coaching, and practice.

Then there's an important bonus. Nothing builds a person's overall self-confidence as much as acquiring the skills to give an effective talk in front of a group. Once you become a comfortable public speaker, the resulting self-confidence will spill over into all aspects of your life, with the result that you will become a more successful and effective person in everything you do.

Poise makes you the master of any situation, and poise can be learned. This book shows you how.

In a nutshell . . .

1. Business presentations cost a lot, both in money and hours.
2. Most business presentations could be vastly improved.
3. People are attracted to articulate, well-organized, forceful speakers.
4. Many people's careers are blocked because of poor speaking skills.
5. Effective speakers will become today's leadership elite.
6. You can't be a real leader if you don't have the power of persuasion.
7. It isn't only businesspeople and professionals who need to be effective speakers.
8. One of life's most rewarding experiences is convincing an audience of your point of view.
9. Public speaking skills can, like any other skill, be acquired through study, coaching, and practice.
10. The confidence gained by becoming an effective public speaker will spill over into all aspects of your life.

THE RIGHT TOPIC

The key to a successful public speaking experience is the right topic, and there is a very effective formula for choosing it. The formula is so effective that if your topic meets all three of its criteria, your success is absolutely guaranteed.

The three criteria are:

1. You must have significant knowledge about the topic you're going to be speaking on.

2. You must sincerely care about the topic you're going to be talking about.

3. You must have a strong desire to impart your knowledge and feelings to your audience.

Dale Carnegie, the patron saint of public speaking training, began using this approach to identify appropriate topics almost a century ago. The way Mr. Carnegie put it was that you must have earned the right to talk about your topic, you must be excited about your topic, and you must be eager to talk about your topic. No one has since developed a better approach.

You've probably seen this formula at work. It might have been a business presentation where the presenter clearly knew the subject well, was fired up about it, and let his enthusiasm spill over to the audience. Maybe it was a fire-and-brimstone sermon that made you sit up and take notice. Or perhaps it was that town meeting where one of your neighbors, who you never thought could make a compelling speech, carried the night by convincing everyone that speed bumps should be installed on your street. Think back to every really effective speech you've ever heard and you'll discover that all the speakers knew their topics inside out, they all felt strongly about what they were talking about, and they all clearly wanted to get their messages across.

If you know everything you need to know about your topic, you'll have enough confidence that distractions, interruptions, or losing your train of thought won't bother you. If you really care about your topic, you won't worry during your delivery about how you look and sound; you'll be too busy concentrating on the message you want the audience to go away with. If you're really looking forward to the opportunity to get your message across, you'll do so with feeling and enthusiasm, and your audience will catch your mood. In short, you'll succeed.

On the other hand, if you try to make a speech on a topic you don't know enough about, you will fail. It's not possible to have a successful speaking experience when you don't know what you're talking about. So, how do you gain enough knowledge about a subject to feel confident it's the right topic? There are two ways: study and experience. If your remarks are based on both these criteria, you will definitely be speaking on the right topic.

People often have trouble deciding at what point their study and experience have sufficiently qualified them to speak about a subject. Well, one reasonable rule of thumb is that if you know more about it than will most of the people in your audience, you're qualified to speak on that topic to that particular group. If most of your listeners know more about the topic than you do, there isn't much you can accomplish (unless, of course, you're bringing a completely new approach or angle).

Don't worry about the possibility of some people in the audience knowing more about your topic, or some aspects of it, than you do. Because you're going to be speaking on something that everyone in the audience is interested in (or, presumably, they wouldn't be there), it could happen that there will be one or two people who know as much about the topic as you do, or more. But that doesn't matter. They will still be interested in hearing your thoughts on the topic; they will be curious about your experiences and how those experiences affect your views. That's why you will often see a panel of three or four speakers all dealing with the same topic; they've all had different experiences and all have different views on the subject matter because of that. Always remember that never in the entire history of the world has there been anyone exactly like you with exactly the same experiences you've had, and, what's more, there never will be. Every experience you've ever had, and every lesson you've ever learned, is a story waiting to be told. All you need is the right audience.

What happens if you have significant knowledge about a topic but your interests have changed and you are no longer excited about it? It's probably a good idea to get someone else to give the talk, but that's not always possible. Perhaps there's no one else available who knows as much as you do about the subject; because significant knowledge is the most important criterion in the topic-selection formula, you have to give the talk. This is when you must act as if you really care about it. Start off your presentation by pretending with all your might that what you're talking about is the most important thing in the world to you at this particular time. If you do, an amazing effect takes place. After a moment or two you'll start to feel the way you're acting. Try it. It works. Act happy and you'll begin to feel happy. Act excited about something and you'll become excited about it. Act as if you care and you'll start to care.

You might also run into the situation where, although you know all you need to about a particular topic and do have an emotional investment in it, you don't particularly want to give the talk. Perhaps you have a conflicting engagement, or maybe you have to travel a long distance to make the presentation. It could be you're just feeling a little lazy. As in the case of not being too excited about a topic, you probably should decline the invitation. But there also may be compelling reasons why you should make the speech.

In these circumstances you must talk yourself into wanting to give the talk. Come to terms with whatever good reasons exist for your taking on the task. Again, it could be that you're the best person to do it, or perhaps you're the only qualified person available at the particular time. It should be easy to convince yourself to give the talk if the person who asked you to give it is important to you, such as your boss, an important client, or a good friend. Maybe the audience really needs to hear about *your* particular experiences and views because they most closely parallel the audience's interests. The point is, much like acting as if you care about your topic will result in your actually beginning to care about it, finding a way to rationalize why you should give this particular talk, at this particular place, at this particular time, to this particular audience will result in your wanting to do it; the third criterion will therefore be met.

If you meet all three of the formula's criteria, success is guaranteed. The confidence generated by a thorough knowledge of your subject, bolstered by your sincere belief in what you're saying, riding on your desire to impart this information and feeling to your audience, creates an unbeatable combination that will render a lackluster presentation impossible.

In a nutshell . . .

1. The key to a successful speaking experience is to be talking about the right topic for you.
2. The topic must be one about which you have significant knowledge.
3. The topic must be one about which you sincerely care.
4. You must have a strong desire to impart your knowledge and feelings to the audience.
5. If you know your material inside out and upside down, you'll perform with such confidence that distractions, interruptions, or losing your train of thought will not be a problem.
6. If you care enough about your topic you won't fall into the trap of worrying, during your delivery, about how you look and sound.
7. If you really want to impart your knowledge and feelings about your topic, you'll have a good time doing so, and the audience will catch your excitement and end up having a good time too.

8. You can sometimes meet the criterion of caring enough about the topic by acting as if you do.

9. You can usually find a way to rationalize wanting to give the talk.

10. If your topic meets all three of the formula's criteria, you couldn't fail even if you wanted to.

11. But if you don't meet the significant knowledge criterion, you will fail.

MANAGING FEAR

The fear of public speaking is real and widespread. It's been said that many people would list public speaking ahead of dying on a list of things they dread most. The bad news is that if this phobia isn't managed effectively it will likely become a self-fulfilling prophecy. The good news is that the feeling is perfectly normal, you can manage it, and, indeed, you can overcome it.

To properly manage the fear of public speaking, you must first understand exactly what it is—nothing more than classic stage fright. It is usually the result of thinking that all of your short-comings are going to become flagrantly evident during this short-term event. The fact is that most of the so-called shortcomings that you're worried about are just figments of your imagination. Even those that might be real are likely being blown out of proportion by an overactive imagination. Don't think that you have to over-come all your weaknesses, whether real or imagined, at once. To counter this temporary anxiety, you must build long-term confidence in your ability to fix what needs to be fixed and learn to place everything else in its proper perspective.

Instead of wasting time and energy worrying about what might go wrong, consider instead what is important right now: you were asked to give this presentation to this particular audience, so at least someone thinks you're the right person for it. Then start to think about how you can best prepare and deliver the speech. This will put things in their proper perspective. You're not putting your life on the line in a half-hour speech. There are about forty-two million minutes in a typical lifetime, so someone's opinion of just thirty of them shouldn't worry you too much. Just as dropping a ball in a game of catch doesn't mean that you lack physical coordination, so stumbling a bit in a speech doesn't mean you're stupid or incompetent. Although it's true that continued bad performances at the lectern can badly damage a career, a subpar performance or two, particularly early in your career as a public speaker, certainly won't ruin your reputation.

But this doesn't mean that the fear doesn't need to be managed, especially in your rookie phase as a public speaker. Even after gaining confidence as a speaker you might need some fear management when you're dealing with a new topic or when you're about to face a particularly daunting audience. So, here's how you prevent your fear from becoming a self-fulfilling prophecy.

Early on you need to remember that you will eventually overcome your fear as you gain experience and acquire and hone the skills needed to become a poised public speaker. In the meantime, the most important aspect of managing your fear is to develop the right mental attitude.

You must start with believing in yourself as a person, believing in the positions you're going to take, and believing that what you have to say is valuable to your audience. Remind yourself that you know enough about the topic to merit the audience's attention.

Convince yourself that you're the right person to make this presentation. This may mean giving yourself a few mental pep talks during your preparation, and at any other time that doubt begins to rear its ugly head. Be sure to give yourself a couple of pep talks before arriving at the podium on the day of the presentation.

Anytime you feel a negative attitude about a presentation creeping in, remind yourself what a proud and satisfying moment it is when you take a stand on an important issue. Then think about what a wonderful feeling it is to convince people that your position is the right one. Remind yourself again that somebody thinks you have something worthwhile to say, or else you wouldn't have been asked to speak.

Remember that even if there are a couple of people in the audience who know a lot about your topic, you have a completely different perspective on it and they'll be interested in hearing your views. You are prepared right now to give any number of talks that no one else could give. That's because no one else has had exactly your experiences, no one else has studied exactly what you have studied, and no one else has developed exactly your attitudes.

Think back to all the times you've approached challenges with feelings of trepidation and I'll bet you'll find that you've almost always surpassed your expectations. Giving a speech is not going to be any different.

Most people's concerns about giving a speech stem from their own expectations, not those of the audience. The audience's expectations are usually a lot lower than your own. This is particularly true in the early stages of your career as a public speaker. Learning to do anything well takes time and effort. No one would expect to play like Oscar Peterson the first time they sit down at a piano, yet many people think they should be able to speak like

Winston Churchill the first time they stand up in front of an audience. There's no such thing as a "natural" speaker. All speakers, even the most accomplished you've ever heard, have had to overcome some level of fear and have acquired their skills and developed their poise over a period of time.

Positive visualization exercises are wonderful therapy for managing the fear of public speaking. Picture yourself being successful in front of the audience and having a really good time giving the talk. See yourself relaxed and smiling. Keep in mind that the audience *wants* you to succeed. They completely sympathize with you because they have, or have had, the same fear of speaking in public as do you.

The greatest weapon against fear, though, is preparation. Spend your time preparing rather than fretting. Concentrate on your message and how you want to deliver it. Think about what you want the audience to learn from your remarks, and stop worrying about yourself. Know your opening (the first minute or two) so well that you can be confident you'll get through it no matter how nervous you feel. Making it through the first few sentences will have an unbelievably settling effect on you.

The second greatest weapon against fear is practice. Be sure to rehearse your speech as often as you can. Then as soon as that speech is out of the way, look for another opportunity to speak in front of a group. The more often you speak publicly, the more comfortable and less fearful you'll become. Join organizations or clubs, get on committees and become involved. Teach Sunday school, join a church group, teach adult classes, become a scout leader, join Toastmasters International. Whether at a company conference or a PTA meeting, grasp any and every opportunity to stand up and say something, even if it's only seconding a motion or stating your agreement or disagreement with something that's just been said.

George Bernard Shaw, in addition to being one of the world's greatest playwrights, also became a successful and much sought-after orator during the golden age of lecture tours. When asked how he developed his public speaking poise, Mr. Shaw is reported to have said, "I did it the same way I learned to skate; by doggedly and repeatedly making a fool of myself until I got used to it." If a great communicator like George Bernard Shaw had to pay his dues by practicing his way through his fear of public speaking, there's no reason for you to be reluctant about doing the same.

If after thorough preparation and a couple of rehearsals you're still overly concerned about your talk, make an appointment with yourself to worry about it. Set aside an hour or so to do nothing but worry about the talk. Make a list of all the things that could possibly go wrong. But instead of simply fretting about them, consider what the odds really are on any of them happening.

You'll quickly realize that most of the things you think could go wrong probably won't, so why worry about them? But don't stop there. Ask yourself what you can do to prevent any potential problems from happening. Then make a note of what action you'd take if something did go awry. At this point it's probably a good idea to throw away the list. Of course, if another appointment with yourself is required you'll need to make a new list, but it likely will be shorter.

Try this and I guarantee that you will get much more comfortable about the speech, even if it takes two or three appointments with yourself. An important by-product of this technique is that on the rare occasion when something you were worrying about actually does happen, you will have rehearsed how to handle it.

When you arrive at the speech venue, remember that physical movement helps offset fear. While sitting at the head table or in the audience waiting your turn, and particularly as your time to speak comes near, there are a few physical things you can do to help alleviate nervousness without making a fool of yourself. You can take some deep breaths. You can clench and unclench your fists (but don't get caught wringing your hands; that always sends a bad signal to the audience). You can squeeze your knees together. You can wiggle your toes.

Remind yourself as you approach the lectern that you should be more concerned about your audience than you are about yourself. When you stand up to speak, stop worrying about how you're going to look and sound. Concentrate instead on your message, remind yourself that you've given this talk a great deal of thought and preparation, that you're the person the audience has come to hear, and that you have something worthwhile to say in which they'll be interested.

Biological reactions to the fear of speaking in front of a group of people are perfectly normal. These reactions include the classic butterflies in the stomach, weak knees, clammy hands, and a tight, dry throat. They will all go away if you ignore them and get on with your task at hand, which is to give the talk. If you forget about your fear and focus instead on your message it will take only a few seconds for the uneasiness to disappear. Once you begin to speak, just concentrate on what you're saying and forget about how you're standing, gesturing, or sounding.

These feelings of anxiety are so natural that if you don't have at least a mild case of them before speaking, you'll probably not give your best performance. What these symptoms really mean is that you care enough about your topic and your audience that you want to do well. Even elite athletes and racehorses get keyed up before events. You should be no different.

Remember that fear is simply a feeling. Following the advice in this chapter may not get rid of the butterflies in your stomach, but it will definitely get them flying in formation.

In a nutshell . . .

1. If you don't manage your fear of public speaking it will likely become a self-fulfilling prophecy.

2. Fear of public speaking is perfectly normal and can be managed and overcome.

3. Maintain a positive, confident attitude about yourself and your message.

4. Give yourself mental pep talks.

5. Visualize yourself giving a successful, well-received speech and having a good time doing it.

6. Audiences tend to be very forgiving toward novice speakers.

7. Objectively assess the odds of something going wrong, and then take the steps necessary to turn those odds in your favor.

8. Even the most accomplished speakers have had to overcome some level of fear early in their careers.

9. The greatest weapon against fear is preparation; prepare rather than fret.

10. The second greatest weapon against fear is practice; the more often you speak in front of groups the less fearful you will be.

Chapter 7

WHAT, WHERE, WHEN, AND TO WHOM

The preparation of your presentation should begin as soon as you are asked to make it. When you are approached to give a talk, find out as much as you can about the sponsoring organization, the event itself, and the venue. Quite often the first approach to a potential speaker is through a third party; for example, it might be someone who knows you personally, but has nothing directly to do with the event. If the person who first contacts you isn't in charge of the program, find out who is running the show and get in touch as soon as possible in order to obtain the information you need to properly prepare.

Your first order of business is to be sure that you know enough about the suggested topic to be able to give an appropriate, informative, and effective talk. To make this assessment you have to be absolutely clear on the organizers' expectations. Don't leave any gray areas. Find out specifically what their expectations are, and be sure you have the necessary knowledge and experience to meet them. Sometimes you'll be able to suggest a slightly different approach that will result in a more comfortable talk for you to give and more useful information for the audience to receive. Suppose that you're an architect and you've been asked to make a presentation to a group of design-and-build contractors on the subject "Why You Should Engage an Architect." This topic might make you sound pretty self-serving and could antagonize some members of the audience. But if the topic is changed to "How an Architect Can Help You Please Your Client," both problems would be solved.

Get all the details about the venue where the event is being held. You need to find out exactly where you're going to be giving the talk, which includes not just the location's address, but which room you're going to be in. You need to find out how big the room is and how it's going to be set up. Find out if there will be a lectern, and get details about the sound system and available audio and visual equipment. Ask where you should park and whom you should look for when you arrive. Getting this information will ensure that you arrive in plenty of time and will reduce unpleasant surprises when you get there. I deliberately use the word *reduce* because there often will be a surprise or two when you arrive to deliver your talk. If something is wrong, don't let it throw you; deal with it and get on with the task at hand, which is to give your talk in as effective a manner as possible.

You should be clear as to the format of the day's program. You need to know:

1. How many people are expected to be in the audience

2. Whether you are the only speaker

3. If there are other speakers, their names, what their topics are, and how to get in touch with them

4. If it's a panel discussion, how to get in touch with the moderator

5. The time of day you are scheduled to speak

6. Where you fit in the order of speakers

7. How much time you have been allotted

8. Whether there is going to be a question and answer period and what its format will be

9. Whether there will be media coverage and what kind it will be

10. Whether you are expected to provide any handout material, how many copies will be required, and who will be responsible for reproducing and distributing them.

Find out exactly what happens immediately before you speak and immediately after you finish. This information may affect your opening and closing remarks. For example, if you're speaking right after someone delivering a talk on a subject related to yours, you should be present to hear that speech. This will ensure that your opening provides an appropriate and smooth transition into your topic. If you're speaking, say, just before a well-known expert on a particular topic, you might want to mention in your closing comments about how much you're looking forward to hearing the next address.

If you are a member of a panel it is a good idea to get in touch with the moderator and the other speakers to ensure that there isn't undue duplication in your presentations. It's worth reminding you here that even if there are three of you dealing with exactly the same topic (which is rare because each speaker on a panel is usually assigned a specific aspect of a broad topic), you shouldn't worry. The audience wants to hear *your* opinions, conclusions, and recommendations resulting from your knowledge and experiences.

But by far your most important task when asked to give a talk is to learn as much as possible about your audience. Different people have different expectations. They think and react differently. They respond to different "hot buttons." What worked wonderfully well in one speaking situation may not do so well in the next. A talk on the taxation of capital gains given to a gathering of lawyers can appropriately focus on the technical aspects of the law, but if your audience is made up of real estate agents you need to make your points in easily understood layperson's terms. The real estate agents are not likely to be interested in the technical wording or the numbers of the sections, subsections, paragraphs, and subparagraphs of the legislation. They'll want to know what transactions are taxed, at what rates, and whether there are ways to eliminate or reduce the tax burden.

So, how do you gain all this knowledge about your audience? Well, you ask questions and engage in research. You can talk to the organizers and to any members of the organization whom you may know personally. You can check the Internet. You can sometimes get the names of people who have previously spoken to the organization and chat with them to get a feel for their experiences. You need to find out what the people you're going to be addressing are talking about these days. What are some of the local issues? All audiences have beliefs, biases, particular interests, and views. Find out as much as you can about them.

Audiences also have particular cultures. Service clubs usually want fairly short, easy-to-understand luncheon addresses. Think tanks, on the other hand, expect their speakers to deliver substantive messages with wide and deep implications. "The Ten Most Common Personal Financial Planning Mistakes" might be a perfect topic for a Rotary club, but an economic club audience would likely be much more interested in the economic growth outlook for the next year. Find out as much as you can about the audience's expectations.

The size of your audience is important. You need a different approach when speaking to a thousand people than when you're going to be addressing an audience of fifty. Five or ten is different still. The larger your audience, the more structured your speech and the more formal your presentation should be. The smaller the group, the less formal and structured you have to be. For example, it would be fine to get into a dialogue with members of an audience of ten; it would be disastrous to do so with an audience of hundreds. For large audiences you will definitely need a lectern and a microphone. For a very small group you could probably get away with sitting on a table holding your notes in your hand.

If you can't get all the information you need about the audience right away, keep asking, right up until you are about to start speaking if necessary. You can usually find out some interesting things about your audience when you arrive at the venue; always arrive early, make yourself available to talk to people, and keep your eyes and ears open for any tidbit that you can use in your talk.

You should always send the organizers the information you want used in your introduction. Don't give them your life history; they might choose the wrong parts of it. Just tell them what's needed to show that you are knowledgeable about your subject, plus anything else that might be relevant to the particular audience. I'm a professional accountant. That fact, and my financial experience, would be important to include in my introduction if I was going to give that talk to the Rotary club mentioned earlier about the ten most common personal financial planning mistakes. But my financial background wouldn't be relevant if I was speaking on how to give an impromptu speech. In this case, it would be my public speaking training, background, and experience that should be highlighted. The fact that I have an honorary degree from the University of Prince Edward Island would be totally irrelevant to a New York audience, but should be included if I was giving a talk somewhere in Atlantic Canada.

In a nutshell . . .

1. When asked to give a talk, find out as much as you can about the organization, the event itself, and the venue.

2. Find out who's in charge of the event and work with that person as much as possible.

3. Be absolutely clear as to what the objectives of the event are.

4. Be sure you understand and agree with the format.

5. Find out what happens immediately before and immediately after you speak so that you can include appropriate comments in your opening and closing remarks.

6. If you're on a panel, get in touch with the moderator and the other speakers to avoid duplication of material.

7. Learn as much as possible about the audience.

8. Provide the organizers with information to be used in your introduction.

BEFORE YOU BEGIN TO WRITE THE SPEECH

The worst-executed part of many presentations is often the preparation stage. There are two reasons for this. The first is that it takes a lot of time to properly prepare a presentation, time which most people wrongly feel they don't really need to spend or have to spare. The second is that most people, even some experienced public speakers, don't really know how to properly prepare a talk. But, as pointed out in this book's introduction, taking the time to properly prepare a presentation might make you or your company more money in one hour than will a year of routine office work—or make the difference between carrying the day or not at your Neighborhood Watch meeting. Proper preparation starts before you actually begin to write your speech.

What Type of Talk?

Most people understand that they have to decide what they're going to say, but few people spend enough time planning how they're going to say it.

You must fully understand the purpose of your presentation. You may simply be informing your audience of something, for instance, if you're explaining how your company's new purchasing procedure works. Some situations call for persuasion, such as convincing your employees that the new purchasing procedure is going to be a good thing for them and the company as a whole. You may be trying to motivate your audience to do something, such as making a presentation to management about why they should introduce a new purchasing procedure. Perhaps you'll be motivating your audience not to do something, possibly speaking to management about delaying introduction of the new purchasing rules until all the bugs are worked out.

The same considerations apply outside of a business context. Suppose you're the treasurer of your local club. You might simply be informing the executive committee of the state of the club's finances. But maybe the finances aren't great, in which case you'd have to persuade the committee that a fee increase is necessary. Then you might have to motivate all the members to vote in favor of increasing the fees when you address them at the annual general meeting.

Decide exactly the type of talk you're going to be giving before you begin to write. To determine the appropriate type of speech, you need to know what the organizer's objectives are and you need to find out as much about your audience as you can, particularly what their expectations are, as outlined in chapter 3, What, Where, When, and to Whom.

There are four basic types of talks:

1. A talk to inform
2. A talk to persuade
3. A talk to motivate
4. A talk to entertain.

Although most of the basics discussed in this book apply to all four types of talks, there are nuances and subtleties attached to each that need to be considered. For some presentations, you will combine two, or perhaps all, of the first three types of talks listed above—to inform, to persuade, and to motivate. But a talk to entertain is simply that: a talk to entertain the audience; nothing more, nothing less.

Never attempt to give a talk to entertain unless the occasion clearly calls for it and you're confident that you have enough interesting, original material to pull it off. This doesn't mean that you shouldn't try to make the other types of talks entertaining, but giving an entertaining talk, which you should always strive for, is totally different than giving a talk designed specifically and solely to entertain. You can make your talks entertaining by following the advice given in this book. Talks to entertain are appropriate at occasions such as retirement parties and wedding receptions.

The best approach for a talk to entertain is to tell stories that involve you and other people in the audience, particularly the guest of honor. A talk to entertain should be filled with details. Tell the audience what happened, who was involved, when it happened, where it all took place, why it happened, and how it all turned out. Name names and describe in detail the people, places, and things involved. If there's a punch line, moral, or interesting twist, keep the mystique alive and don't reveal it until the very end.

A talk to inform is designed to do just that; the audience should leave the room knowing more about the subject than they did when they arrived. All talks, except talks to entertain, are at their core talks to inform.

A talk to persuade involves both imparting information to the audience and persuading them to your point of view. You have to convince the audience that what you're propounding is right and that they should agree with you. To convert a talk to inform to a talk to persuade, you have to introduce unequivocal, easily understandable, relevant, and compelling evidence to back up your points.

A talk to motivate your audience to do or not do something requires at least two and possibly three more ingredients. The first additional ingredient is that you have to clearly tell the audience what you want them to do or not do. The second additional ingredient is that you have to tell them in no uncertain terms what will happen to them if they do or don't do what you're suggesting. The third additional ingredient is to make it as easy as possible for the audience to do what you want them to do, if it's within your power to help them.

Suppose, for example, that you want an audience of one hundred fellow citizens to write to your town council to convince it that a new set of traffic lights is needed in your neighborhood. You should have twenty clipboards, each with a copy of a letter outlining the request, at the back of the room. Have five ballpoint pens beside each clipboard. Tell the audience that all they have to do is sign one of the letters and that you'll look after collecting and mailing them. Explain that because there are twenty copies available, there should be no long lines on the way out. Oh yes, also tell them that, after they sign the letter, they can keep the pen, and make it a good pen not a cheap one. People love to get something, even of modest value, for nothing.

The difference between persuading and motivating is that a talk to persuade may convince your audience that they probably should or shouldn't do something, but a talk to motivate will inspire them to actually do or not do it.

In the simplest terms possible, talks to inform, persuade, and motivate can be illustrated as follows.

A talk to impart information: There is a flight to Chicago at 5:30 this evening with space available.

A talk to persuade: There is a flight to Chicago at 5:30 this evening and you should book it because it's the only remaining flight that has space available.

A talk to motivate: The only flight to Chicago this evening with space available leaves at 5:30 and you should be on it, otherwise you'll have to stay here overnight at your own expense. You need to leave for the airport right now. There's a bus waiting for you at the front entrance. I've already booked your tickets and Tony Meredith—stand up and identify yourself, Tony—will distribute them to you on the way to the airport.

The Right Length

There are a few rules of thumb that will ensure that your presentation is the right length.

The most important guideline is to keep your talk as short as possible. Say only what is absolutely necessary in order to meet the objective of the presentation and the expectation of the audience. Provided these are met, there is no such thing as a speech that's too short. Lincoln's Gettysburg Address contained only two hundred and sixty-eight words. I was in the audience at a Junior Achievement convention in Washington, D.C a number of years ago when the legendary actor John Wayne gave a memorable and convincing luncheon speech that lasted less than two minutes. The impact of the Gettysburg Address is still being felt today, and I doubt that any of the two thousand people who heard John Wayne that day have forgotten his message.

After-dinner presentations should never be more than twenty minutes long. After a cocktail, a nice dinner, and some fine wine, your audience's attention span simply will not tolerate anything longer. Even if your talk might provoke some questions, don't have a question and answer period at the end of an after-dinner speech. The twin dangers of running overtime and having to cut off some people far outweigh any advantage of having a question and answer period. Instead, offer to stay around after your talk to discuss any questions that individual members of the audience might have.

A luncheon speech should ideally be thirty to forty-five minutes long, including the question and answer period, should you decide to have one. Having a question and answer period after a luncheon presentation is perfectly in order provided you don't go beyond the scheduled adjournment time.

Finally, always plan to finish earlier than the audience expects. The show business adage of "leave them wanting more" is just as relevant in public speaking as it is on the stage. Time flies at the lectern, so you'll probably speak longer than you intend to. Prepare material for about 80 percent of your allotted time. This will give you time to deal with any unforeseen delays as well as allow you to finish early and leave them wanting more. You'll probably even get asked back.

It's the Audience That Matters

Before writing your speech, ask yourself what need your audience is hoping to fulfill by coming to hear you, and then logically appeal to that need. You must give the audience something to take away with them.

To determine the appropriate type of talk and the approach you're going to take, you need to ask yourself the following questions:

1. Why have I been asked to address this particular audience?
2. What do they expect from me?
3. What can they learn from my experience and knowledge?
4. What, if anything, do I have in common with them?
5. Does the audience have any problems for which I have the solutions?
6. Is there anything in particular that I think they should or should not do?
7. How much do they know about the subject?

Don't be too quick to dismiss ideas that come into your mind while considering these questions. What's old hat to you may be an interesting revelation to your audience. Anything you remember about your topic may in some way be meaningful, so jot it all down. It's a lot easier at the editing stage to cut out material than it is to add meaningful information.

You are going to be judged on what you say and how you say it; although you want people to remember your name and face, your ultimate responsibility is to see that your message finds its way into the minds of your audience. The best way to get people to remember you is by ensuring that your message makes a strong impact on them. For your message to be memorable, you have to prepare and present your remarks from your audience's point of view.

No matter how strongly you feel about a subject, and no matter how much you want to talk about it, you have to make it mean something to the people sitting there listening to you. Your audience will have formed some sort of expectation about what they're going to hear. You need to find out before you prepare your talk what that expectation is, because they might be in the mood for one type of message but not for another. For example, when introducing that new purchasing procedure to the staff it is best to highlight how their jobs are going to be made easier rather than focusing on the training and overtime necessary to get everything running smoothly.

If there's any chance that the audience might be antagonistic (and they might be mildly antagonistic about something as simple as mandatory attendance at your talk), the more important it is for you to find common ground with them. Find objectives that you share with the audience and then develop points on which they can agree with you. Assume again that you're the treasurer of your club and you're faced with having to inform your fellow club members of a proposed increase in annual dues. It would be a good idea to emphasize the pride that you all have in the club, remind your fellow members how everyone enjoys using attractive and up-to-date facilities, and stress the desirability of maintaining the club's stellar reputation. You should introduce such common ground in the opening of your talk.

Remember, it's always all about the audience. If it's a talk to inform, the audience has to leave knowing more about the topic than they did when they arrived. If it's a talk to persuade, they have to be convinced that you are right. If it's a motivational talk, they have to be inspired to act. If it's a talk to entertain, they have to be amused.

Some Other Considerations

Think about whether you will have to spend time clearing up misconceptions. If the shareholders at an annual general meeting think that their company's performance is not up to industry standards when in fact it is, the CEO better get that misconception out of the way emphatically and immediately.

You can't effectively talk about more than one thing at a time, so it's usually best to stick to one strong message and leave it at that, no matter how powerful the temptation may be to throw in a couple of ancillary thoughts. However, you can talk about a number of different points as long as each one is linked directly to the one strong message. If you can't express the overall theme of your presentation on the back of a business card, it's probably too complex and needs to be reworked and streamlined.

Also keep in mind that although the topic, the theme, and your main points may stay the same for different audiences, one approach may not suit all audiences. Your script and delivery should vary depending on the formality and the mood of the event. If you're promoting changes to make income tax laws easier to understand, you would use different examples when addressing an audience of corporate chief financial officers than you would when speaking to a meeting of the American Association of Retired Persons. Winston Churchill, who often peppered his speeches in the British House of Commons with humor, maintained a perfectly serious tone when delivering his famous Iron Curtain speech. Franklin Delano Roosevelt often used a folksy, down-to-earth tone in his talks, but his "nothing-to-fear-but-fear-itself" address was forceful and compelling.

Finally, before you begin to write your speech, there are two things you need to decide before all others: how you're going to start and how you're going to finish. You might be able to survive a presentation with a soft middle, but you absolutely need a strong opening and a strong closing. If your opening is weak you will lose your audience right away. If your closing is weak you may undo all the positive results you achieved during the earlier part of your speech. Extra time spent on deciding your opening and closing remarks will also make writing the middle part of your presentation a lot easier.

If you've given sufficient thought to all the points in this chapter, you're now ready to begin writing your speech.

In a nutshell . . .

1. There are four types of talks: talks to inform, to persuade, to motivate, and to entertain.

2. Decide which type of talk, or combination of types, you're going to give.

3. The best way to give a talk to entertain is to tell detailed stories involving you and other people in the room, especially a guest of honor.

4. If you're giving a talk to inform, the audience must leave knowing more about the subject than they did when they arrived.

5. To raise the level of a talk to inform to a talk to persuade you have to introduce unequivocal, easily understandable, and compelling evidence to back up your points.

6. In a talk to motivate you have to clearly tell the audience what you want them to do or not do; tell them what will happen to them otherwise; and make it as easy as possible for them to follow your advice.

7. The organizer's objectives and the audience's expectations must be met.

8. After-dinner speeches shouldn't be longer than twenty minutes.

9. Don't have a question and answer period after an after-dinner speech, but it's a good idea to offer to stay around and answer questions after the formal proceedings end.

10. Luncheon speeches shouldn't exceed forty-five minutes, including the question and answer period.

11. Remember it's always good to leave the audience wanting more; plan to finish before the time for adjournment.

12. At this stage of your preparation don't dismiss any thoughts that you feel could be included; it's easier to cut out than add in when editing.

13. If there's even the slightest chance that the audience might be antagonistic, search hard for common ground and points on which they'll agree with you and use these points in your opening.

14. It's usually best to stick to one strong message; if you can't express the theme of your talk on the back of a business card it's probably too complex.

→

→

15. Your script and delivery should vary depending on the formality and expectations of the audience.

16. If misconceptions need to be cleared up, do so during your opening.

17. Your opening and closing are the most important parts of any presentation.

WRITING THE SPEECH

Someone once remarked that the strongest memory is weaker than the palest ink. Only an egomaniac would rely completely on memory for a speech of any length, and only the misguided try to develop talking notes without first writing out the entire speech.

There are five good reasons you should always write out your entire speech:

1. It is the only way to ensure that you develop a consistent message.

2. You can time how long it takes to read it using appropriate pacing and emphasis. (The most accurate way to check the timing is by rehearsing with a stopwatch.)

3. It's easier to edit and organize a written script than to continuously change and juggle notes.

4. It's easier to decide whether, and where in the presentation, to use visual aids when you're working with a script.

5. Even if you eventually speak from notes, writing out the speech in its entirety helps you develop your material sufficiently to be completely confident at the lectern.

Begin your first draft by putting down all your thoughts without worrying about length. You will then go back and edit, refine, and re-edit until you have a script that you're reasonably comfortable with. It's doubtful that you'll ever come up with a script that *completely* satisfies you. You'll probably want to make a change or two every time you look at it. It's not unusual for experienced speakers to make changes to their notes while sitting at the head table waiting to be introduced.

Choose Your Words Carefully

You have to make the material your own. Even busy, top-level executives who have speechwriters should participate in the writing of their speeches; the greater the level of participation the better. The best way to ensure that the speech sounds like you is to write the speech as if you were talking to a group of friends, and this means that you have to talk while you're writing. Remember that the audience is going to hear your words, not read them. Speak the words out loud so that you know how they will sound to the audience as well as how they look to you. To be heard naturally a speech has to be written naturally.

There are two elements that make a presentation effective and convincing. One is the speaker's emotional investment in the subject; the other is the logic of the presentation. You have to capture in words the essence of your thoughts and feelings. Immerse yourself completely in the substance of what you want to say and the words will come. Never feel uncomfortable about using words that let your feelings show through.

Your talk has to be easy for the audience to follow, understand, and remember. The unknown has to be related to the known and the mysterious must be demystified, which is where the power of analogies, metaphors, illustrations, and examples comes in. Use simple language that everyone in the audience can understand. Ask yourself, "Will the audience understand what this means?" Buzzwords and jargon should be avoided as much as possible, unless they are part of the language of the audience. But jargon is useful in particular contexts, usually as shorthand for a more complex expression. So, if using a buzzword or two will make your talk clearer, by all means do so. But never assume that an audience knows what a term means; always clearly define it the first time you use it.

Unless speaking to peers on a technical subject, an engineer shouldn't sound like an engineer; an accountant should take great pains not to sound like an accountant; and a lawyer should never sound like a lawyer. Your presentation is an event that you're writing a script for, not a textbook.

Language that is anything other than simple and conversational will get in the way of the message. As already mentioned, you must sound natural, and the secret to sounding natural is to speak in a conversational tone. The audience has to understand your words as well as hear your voice. For example, say, "I'll keep you up to date" rather than, "further notification will follow in due course." Instead of saying, "Appropriate amendments will be introduced in a timely fashion," tell the audience exactly what you're going to do and when you're going to do it. "A person's desire for possession of material goods will, on occasion, overwhelm one's innate sense of prudence" is a very elegant sentence. However, you're far more apt to get your message across by saying, "Greed often prevails over common sense."

Anytime you catch yourself saying "in other words" you can delete whatever came just before. Obviously it wasn't clear enough.

Never use words that you have difficulty pronouncing. If you have trouble saying "linoleum," say "floor covering" instead. If "brewery" is a tongue twister for you, construct the sentence so that you can humorously say, "the place where they make the beer."

A picture is, indeed, worth a thousand words. Poets know this, which is why their works live on for eons. So, paint word pictures. Don't just say, "The dog." Say, "The shaggy little black poodle with soulful brown eyes and perfect posture." If you don't paint clear images in their minds, the audience will come up with their own images; what they conjure up may not fit the image you're trying to create or the message you're trying to convey.

Use impact words:

- *Smashed* is stronger than *broken.*
- *Thrilled* is more descriptive than *happy.*
- *Weary* is more emphatic than *tired.*
- *Magnificent* is more impressive than *very good.*
- *Sweltering* is a vast improvement on *very warm.*
- Whenever you're tempted to use the word *very,* you should look for a more descriptive word.

Alliteration and repetition, if not overdone, can add force to a presentation. Politicians are particularly adept at this. For example, "We can't continually coddle criminals" is a lot catchier than "We must cease being soft on lawbreakers." I once heard a politician effectively establish his pacing by using the word *great* four times in a twenty-one word sentence: "It's great to be standing before this great audience in this great city of Nashville, in this great state of Tennessee."

You should always have a dictionary and a thesaurus at hand while writing your speech. Time spent searching for the right word is always worth it. Discovering the perfect word will not only enliven your public speaking style, but will also help you develop an expanded vocabulary. This, in turn, will improve your conversational skills and make your memos, letters, and emails much more effective. The more you expand your vocabulary, the less time you'll have to spend searching for the right word or phrase.

Pronouns

The overuse of third-person pronouns will always create problems for the audience. While you may be fully aware of what the antecedents are, the audience may have a terrible time trying to figure it out. Suppose you're halfway through an update to your board of directors on negotiations with suppliers and you throw in this sentence:

> "He told him that he or I would be happy to meet with either of them."

Don't be too surprised if the board misses completely that you really meant:

> "Our executive vice president, Larry Sinclair, called David Collier, Newcorp's vice president of operations, offering to have either Larry or me meet with David, or with Mary Carlisle, their new CEO, whichever they preferred."

Dialogue

An often overlooked technique in writing a speech is the use of dialogue. Suppose you were reporting back to your PTA on a meeting you had with the chair of the board of school trustees. Don't just say:

> "I told her of our concerns and she expressed very little interest. Even after I pressed her a bit I didn't have any success."

Say it this way:

> "I said to Ms. Henry, 'Ms. Henry, we are very worried that your board is not allocating enough money for school supplies in District 3.'
>
> "Ms. Henry said, 'Well, every district would like more money.'
>
> "I handed her our document and said, 'I'm sure that's true, but here is a list of items that District 3 teachers had to purchase out of their own pockets.'
>
> "All she said was, 'Thank you.'
>
> "I pressed on, saying, 'Ms. Henry, this is a very serious problem that needs to be addressed right away.'
>
> "She dismissed me by saying, 'Well, thank you for taking the time to come in.'
>
> "Even when I asked, 'Will you be bringing this to the attention of the board?' all I got in reply was, 'I guess so.'"

Note how quoting the dialogue more accurately illustrates and conveys the tone and futility of the conversation than does the bland, general description.

Be Positive Rather Than Negative

It's usually more persuasive to talk about what you are for rather than what you're against. Audiences tend to relate more favorably to positive, enthusiastic speakers than they do to sour-sounding whiners and complainers.

Let's suppose you're making a pitch for the government to simplify the income tax law. It'd be more effective to craft your speech using examples of the positive effects of tax simplification rather than negative examples of leaving the law as it is.

Use examples such as:

1. More people being able to complete and file their own income tax returns, thereby saving money on professional fees

2. Money saved by government through lower administration costs

3. More respect from the general public for the tax laws.

Rather than examples such as:

1. How upset and confused people get over filing their tax returns

2. The extra costs to individuals of having professionals prepare and file their tax returns

3. The additional government administration costs resulting from overly complex legislation.

Also, it's always better to affirm your own views rather than attack someone else's. You'll be more persuasive telling people why you are right than why someone else is wrong. An audience needs to know that you believe strongly in what you're saying, not just that you disagree with someone else's point of view.

Use the Active Voice and Short Sentences

The active voice is always more powerful than the passive voice. For example, "The hard-hit baseball shattered the huge plate glass window" conjures up a much stronger image than, "The big window was broken by a ball."

Short sentences tend to be more effective than long, drawn-out sentences because they require less of the audience's concentration. Remember that your words are going to be heard, not read, so the audience can't go back and take a second look. Compare the two sentences below and consider which is more likely to be understood and remembered by an audience:

1. Many of the people in this room will have tremendous difficulty retaining ownership and possession of their current habitation if the imbalance among the various tax bases on which taxes paid by individuals are levied is not addressed in a timely manner by the traditional levels of taxing authorities.

2. If the city keeps increasing our property taxes in order to levy a lower sales tax, many of us will soon lose our homes.

Now let's look at how powerful the combination of a short sentence and the active voice can be. Again, compare the two examples below:

1. Many more war materials must be made available to those of us on this side of the water in order for us to proceed militarily to the ultimate denouement of the daunting task of defeating our intractable enemy.

2. Give us the tools and we will finish the job.

(This second sentence is, of course, the powerful, inspirational, and effective way that Winston Churchill conveyed to Franklin

Delano Roosevelt the Allies' dire need for American help during World War II.)

Believe it or not, the two long-winded examples above, and other such examples given throughout this book, are not exaggerations. Many speakers actually talk like that.

Organization

If what you say is complex, mixed-up, or vague, the audience is going to tune out. Your talk must be logically organized and easy to follow. You should speak not just so the audience can understand you, but also so that they cannot misunderstand you. Depend on the fact that if something *can* be misunderstood, it *will* be misunderstood.

One of the oldest suggestions in the history of public speaking is "tell them what you're going to tell them, tell them, and then tell them what you told them." This usually works provided you understand that it does not mean giving the same talk three times. It means that you tell the audience in a sentence or two what the talk is going to be about, then you make your points and present your evidence, and finally you clearly summarize the message you want them to take away.

Following is how this approach would work when giving a talk on the ten most common financial planning mistakes:

1. Your opening comments could be, "Good afternoon, ladies and gentlemen. For the next thirty minutes or so I'm going to outline the ten most common personal financial planning mistakes that people make." (Tell them what you're going to tell them.)

2. You would then outline in detail, with lots of examples and illustrations, the ten mistakes. (Tell them.)

> **3.** You would close with, "There you have it, ladies and gentlemen, the ten most common personal financial planning mistakes. They are . . ." and you would then list them in point form with no editorial comment whatsoever. (Tell them what you told them.)

To make sure your speech is well organized, write down all your thoughts, cut out the confusing parts, and then arrange what's left in a logical order based on the type of talk you're going to be giving, which in turn should be based on the organizer's objectives and the audience's expectations.

Plan your bridges, segues, and transitions. You know where you've been, you know where you are, and you know where you're going with your message. Although an audience may know where you've just been and where you are, they have no idea what's coming next, so be sure it all ties together. You need to use bridges such as "so those are the causes of the problem"; "now I'm going to suggest some solutions for you to consider"; and "finally, what you need to do, ladies and gentlemen, is . . ." These types of phrases will help you keep an audience on the same page with you.

To keep yourself on track, ask yourself these kinds of questions while you are drafting your speech:

1. What point am I making here?

2. Is it important to this audience?

3. Why is it important to them?

4. What are some solutions to the audience's problems?

5. Which solution should I suggest?

6. How can I best back up my recommendation?

Considering what the audience already knows is extremely well advised; there truly is little need to preach to the choir. However, it's dangerous to *assume* what your audience knows or doesn't know. As emphasized in chapter 4, Before You Begin to Write the Speech, if you didn't determine the level of your audience's knowledge of your topic when asked to give the talk, you have to take the time to find out before starting to write the speech.

Ask yourself, "Could somebody else give this *exact* speech?" If the answer is yes, scrap what you've done and start over, putting more of your own experiences, opinions, and recommendations into it. If you hired someone to write the speech, you wouldn't accept excuses for a poorly thought-out and poorly prepared presentation, so why should you accept one from yourself?

Evidence

To persuade audiences to agree with you you have to back up your assertions with clear evidence. This is where relevant illustrations, examples, and analogies come in, as do the stories based on your experience and knowledge that earned you the right to make the talk. The evidence you use to bring the audience around to your point of view is the most important content in a talk to persuade. Most speeches fail in this, and when they do it is usually because the speaker was too lazy during preparation to give it the thought and consideration that it requires.

Relate the strange to the familiar. Look for analogies and similar situations when introducing a new topic to an audience. Compare your point to something the audience is familiar with, something that they already understand. Doing so will help them better grasp your point and will usually make them more receptive to your message. For example, if you're trying to convince people to use online banking, it could be pointed out that doing so is as easy as sending an email. This is another example of why finding out as much as you can about your audience is so important. *You* need to know what *they* need to know.

Contrasts can often be effective, such as comparing a 50 percent increase in crime to a 10 percent cutback in police patrols. Be sure any data you use are accurate, relevant, and the most current available. Talking about the latest developments always enhances your credibility and authority.

Your evidence must be presented in terms that are relevant to the particular audience. There's not much point in introducing gross national product statistics to an audience of senior citizens who came out to hear why their property taxes are increasing. On the other hand, gross national product statistics may be exactly what you need in a presentation to a government department.

It's important not to overwhelm your audience with so much supporting evidence that it becomes forgettable. Two or three strong points are a lot better than ten mediocre points, but be sure you have enough to be convincing. Because examples teach, and almost nothing else does, you should turn abstract thoughts into concrete examples. "There were twenty-six more murders and two hundred and six more robberies this year than last year" is a lot more effective than "Crime is on the rise." But, again, you must use relevant examples. The statement that 99.9 percent of people killed in car accidents in Philadelphia last year had bathrooms in their homes may be absolutely accurate, but it's pretty hard to identify its relevance to anything.

To establish your points you have to argue, clarify, elaborate, and support, but don't preach. By "preach" I mean talking down to an audience, adopting a tone that says, "I know a lot more about this than you do so you better listen to what I say." Preaching rarely persuades. Indeed, preaching usually turns the audience against you, which, of course, is the exact opposite of the end you want to achieve.

Quotations

Quotations can be used effectively to demonstrate that other people, often people with a lot more credibility than you have, share your views.

As with examples, quotations must be relevant and the source should be authoritative. If the person you're quoting isn't well known to your audience, you have to briefly state his or her qualifications. Don't ever rely on memory to accurately recall a quotation.

Don't paraphrase; always, without exception, read the quotation verbatim. Write the quotation out in full, noting the source and the source's qualifications, if necessary.

Use Specific Details

In a talk to inform, the information has to be presented in a way that's easily understood. Saying, "There are limitations on the dimensions of a storage shed you can erect in your backyard," is not very informative. You need to set out for the audience, in easily understood terms, exactly what those limitations are, such as, "You can't have a storage shed in your backyard taller than fourteen feet or less than fifteen feet from your property line."

"We had one hundred and eight emails, twenty letters, and forty telephone calls" is much more informative and convincing evidence than "We received numerous responses." Don't just say, "We have to make a greater investment in our marketing efforts if we want to increase revenue significantly." A little research should enable you to say, "We're confident that an increase of two hundred thousand dollars in our marketing budget will result in an increase in sales of over a million dollars."

"Now is the time for all good men to come to the aid of the party" has a nice motivational ring to it, but as an informative statement it needs to be followed up with the more specific, "We each have to go out and sign up six new members before the end of the month."

If your purpose is to persuade your audience, then you have to present concrete evidence to support your premise rather than just general data. In fact, in a talk to persuade, you have a responsibility to your audience to reach specific conclusions, make it perfectly clear what those conclusions are, and then present clear, relevant evidence to back up your position.

Suppose you're trying to convince your city council that a traffic light is needed at the corner of Elm Avenue and Maple Street. Don't just say:

> "A lot of people agree with me that there are too many accidents at the corner of Elm and Maple and that something needs to be done. It's been proven that the installation of traffic lights reduces accidents."

What you should say is:

> "Over the past five years, an average of twenty-three traffic accidents per year have happened at the intersection of Elm Avenue and Maple Street. During that time there have been eighteen serious injuries and four people have died; two of them pedestrians.

"The intersection of Connaught Street and Richmond Avenue is similar in every respect to Elm and Maple. There is about the same amount of traffic and the neighborhoods are practically identical.

"During the three-year period after the installation of traffic lights at Connaught and Richmond, there were 90 percent fewer traffic accidents, there were no serious injuries, no fatalities, and only one pedestrian was involved in a traffic mishap."

Don't just say:

"Something really has to be done about the problem at Elm and Maple."

What you should say is:

"The intersection of Elm and Maple is a very dangerous one that is threatening the safety and lives of anyone who passes through it, and most of the people who pass through it live in our city, just like you and me.

"Something must be done about this situation before the next victim is one of you, one of your neighbors, or one of your children.

"It's clear to me, and to the two thousand people who have signed the petition I'm about to present to you, that the solution is to have traffic lights installed at Elm and Maple."

In a talk to motivate, you also have to make clear recommendations as to what you want the audience to do or not do. You have to give specific examples of what's at risk, the consequences of doing nothing, and what you want your audience to do about it.

When you were addressing your neighborhood ratepayers' association to get the signatures on the petition to city council mentioned above, you wouldn't have gotten two thousand of them by saying:

> "We can't let the authorities continue with such indifference."

To get two thousand signatures, you would have had to present the same evidence and data that you presented to city council, and then close by saying something like:

> "We need to convince our city council that traffic lights are an absolute necessity at Elm and Maple. Accidents will continue to occur and people will continue to be injured, possibly killed, possibly one of us who is in this very hall tonight; possibly one of our loved ones. We can no longer allow the city council to ignore this very serious situation. If you care about yourselves, your family, your friends, and your neighbors, then you must sign one of the copies of the petition at the back of the hall."

Specific examples and details are the keys to believability, and believability and clarity are the keys to persuasion and motivation.

The Takeaway

A takeaway is a catchy phrase or a great line that makes a speech unforgettable. Even a mediocre speech can be turned into a memorable message by the use of a powerful takeaway.

Would the whole world have remembered these words: "The Soviet Union has taken control of Eastern Europe"? Not likely. But Churchill's "from Stettin in the Baltic to Trieste in the Adriatic, an iron curtain has descended across the continent" will never be forgotten.

Would people still remember President Kennedy's words had he said, "We need to rethink how we interact with government" rather than, "Ask not what your country can do for you; ask what you can do for your country"? No, they would not.

Here are some more examples of memorable takeaways:

1. "That's one small step for man, one giant leap for mankind." Neil Armstrong.

2. "If the glove doesn't fit, you must acquit." Johnnie Cochran, O. J. Simpson's lawyer.

3. "Forgive your enemies, but never forget their names." John F. Kennedy.

4. "The only thing we have to fear is fear itself." Franklin Delano Roosevelt.

You're not going to come up with a great takeaway for every speech you make, but they are so effective that you should always spend some time trying to develop one.

Opening

It's rare for the audience not to be completely with you at the beginning of your presentation, and it's always a lot easier to keep an audience's attention than it is to get it back. Therefore, your opening is the most critical part of your talk. You simply cannot afford to lose your audience during your first few sentences.

It's always an honor to be asked to address an audience, so let them know that you recognize and appreciate that. If there is any reason why you're especially pleased to speak to a particular group, be sure to tell them about it. For example, if I were giving a talk to a Shriners club I would certainly say how honored I was to be associated, even in a small way, with an organization that's done so much for children over such a long period of time.

An effective way to open a talk is to compliment your audience on something that they will be surprised you know about. For example, if you're speaking to the oldest Lions club in the country, let them know that you know this, and congratulate them on the fact.

Find out what most of the audience members have in common and search for a way to fit yourself in. It may be something as simple as your having once lived in their city. Or perhaps your father had been a member of the organization and you have fond memories of how proud he was of their accomplishments. Look particularly for common goals that you may share with the audience. Your objective should be to have them thinking, "Gosh, I didn't realize we had so much in common."

Opening with a surprising fact, as long as it isn't overly dramatic, can be effective. Suppose you're giving a talk to a group of young professionals on the importance of having disability insurance. A good opener would be:

> "The odds are, ladies and gentlemen, that any one of you in this room is more likely to become disabled than die before the age of sixty-five. So, why do you have life insurance and no disability insurance?"

That opener will focus the audience's thinking in the direction that you desire. On the other hand, if you opened your talk by dramatically asking them to visualize themselves not being able to perform everyday tasks of living, they'd probably end up thinking about the horrors that may befall them rather than about the advantages of disability insurance.

A few more words of caution on openers are warranted.

Never voluntarily mention that you've given the same speech before, even if it was two thousand miles away and six months ago.

Each audience wants to be special, so don't spoil the feeling for them. On the other hand, if asked, never deny that you have given essentially the same talk before.

Never start with a joke. There are three compelling reasons for this particular caution:

1. The odds are pretty good that some, if not all, of the audience will already have heard it, especially these days with the proliferation of jokes on the Internet.

2. Unless you're a master storyteller you probably won't enhance your reputation as a speaker by starting with a joke. Most people, contrary to their own beliefs, are not very good joke-tellers.

3. No matter how benign the joke may be, in this era of heightened political correctness, there's a real chance that someone in the audience will be offended. As mentioned above, the audience is usually completely on your side at the start of a talk, so why do anything that might cause you to lose even one of them?

Now, I'm not suggesting that you never use humor, but it should be humor that's relevant to your content and that presents itself spontaneously, either while you're preparing the talk or while you're delivering it.

Finally, spend no more than a few moments identifying with the audience as outlined above and then get on with the heart of your presentation. Start strongly. Make sure that the beginning of your formal content is relevant to your subject and is appropriate to the audience and the setting. You want the audience to be interested in hearing more of what you have to say; you do not want them deciding that they should have stayed at the office.

Closing

Because your closing is the last thing the audience will hear you say, it has to be equally as strong as your opening. A technique that seldom fails is to briefly summarize your main points. But be careful not to repeat major portions of your speech. A closing summary should always be in point form. Just succinctly repeat your points and resist the temptation to elaborate.

In a talk to motivate, if you don't ask you probably won't get. You have to let your audience know exactly and clearly what it is that you want them to do or not do. Then you have to remind them what the consequences of action or inaction will be.

A closing technique that is very effective when appropriate is the call to action. Another effective closing technique is to take a peek into the future, something such as:

> "So, you see, ladies and gentlemen, if we don't take steps now to plan and finance an expansion of our seniors' facilities, as more and more people continue to live longer they will have no comfortable places in which to reside and not enough trained professionals to look after them."

Don't be subtle when making important closing points. Use a sledgehammer! Don't say:

> "This tax increase will have a negative effect on some people."

Say:

> "This outrageous money grab by the government will, for many of us in this room, cause our mothers and fathers and uncles and aunts to lose their homes!"

If you were fortunate enough to come up with a great takeaway, always use it emphatically in your closing.

The Script Itself

There are seven critical rules for typing a final script:

1. It's always better to have a lot of pages than to have a script that's too small or disorganized to read.

2. Be sure the type size is large enough for you to read comfortably.

3. Use upper- and lowercase letters, regardless of the type size.

4. The last sentence on a page must end on that page.

5. The text should be double spaced, with a triple space between paragraphs.

6. Use only the top three-quarters of each page. This will prevent you from dropping your head too low and helps you maintain eye contact with the audience.

7. Number your pages on all four corners. This will make putting them back in order a lot easier should you drop them or they otherwise get mixed up.

There's no reason to worry about whether your speech looks nice on paper; you just want it to be readable. It's how it sounds to the audience that counts.

Five Rules for When You Think You're Finished

1. Go over your speech one more time and edit ruthlessly.

2. Eliminate all redundancies, except repetitions which were put in deliberately for effect.

3. Although details make a talk come alive, too many details can obscure clarity, so don't overdo it; be sure every detail adds something to the message or necessarily reinforces a point.

4. Stay within your capabilities; if you're not absolutely certain about what you're saying, don't say it.

5. To make your talk sound right, after the script is typed you should mark it up with delivery cues, such as underlines, double underlines, exclamation marks, slashes for phrasing, double slashes for pause points, and anything else that works for you.

Writing a Speech for Someone Else

The rules, techniques, and advice contained in this book apply equally to writing a speech for someone else as they do to writing your own speech. However, there is an important added complication: how do you make a speech sound like someone else?

When it comes to writing words that others are going to make their own, it's a lot easier to describe what has to be done than it is to do it. You have to learn their favorite words, their style of phrasing, and the types of illustrations and examples they like to use. Not only do you have to write like they sound, but you also have to write like they think.

The difficulty of your task will depend in large part on your relationship with the person for whom you're writing the speech and how much experience you have writing for that particular person. The better you get to know a person and that person's style, the easier your writing will be.

Two questions you should always ask a person for whom you're writing a speech are:

1. What's the central message that you want the audience to take away?

2. What type of talk do you want it to be: to inform, to persuade, to motivate, or a combination thereof?

You will notice that a talk to entertain is not included here. Unless you're a professional comedy writer, it's not a good idea to write a speech to entertain for someone else. It's perfectly in order to help them with it, say by reviewing the script or listening to the speech and offering suggestions, but speeches to entertain rely so heavily on personal content that people should always write their own.

In a nutshell . . .

1. You should always write out your speech in full even if you're going to be speaking from notes.

2. Make the material your own; write it as if you were talking. Your words are to be heard, not read.

3. Never feel uncomfortable about using words that let your feelings show through.

4. Use simple language.

5. Make your words and phrases human rather than institutional.

6. Never use words you have difficulty pronouncing.

7. Don't be afraid to use dialogue.

8. Whenever you have a choice, be positive rather than negative.

9. Support your positions rather than attack other people's.

10. Use short sentences, the active voice, and powerful words.

11. Always have a dictionary and a thesaurus at hand while writing your speech.

→

→

12. Organize your material not only to be understood but also so that it cannot be misunderstood.

13. Be sure your illustrations and examples are clear, persuasive, and relevant.

14. Be specific; specifics make speeches come alive. Generalizations make for dull speeches.

15. Don't overuse illustrations and examples to the point where the audience becomes confused.

16. Have a strong opening. Grasp the audience's attention right away.

17. Have an equally strong closing. Make a concerted effort to find a catchy phrase or line that will make the speech memorable.

18. When you think you're finished writing your speech, ruthlessly edit it one more time.

19. Mark up your final script or notes with delivery cues.

20. Recognize that there are particular requirements to be met when writing a speech for someone else.

VISUAL AIDS

The range of available visual aids stretches all the way from a flip chart costing a few dollars to professional audiovisual productions costing tens of thousands of dollars. Many books have been written, and many courses designed, dealing with the production and presentation of audiovisual shows.

This book is about gaining poise and confidence as a speaker; it is designed to help you develop into a dynamic presenter rather than a graphic arts designer or a computer technician. Therefore, this chapter will simply deal with some principles to keep in mind when deciding whether to use visual aids, how many to use, and how to use them effectively.

Unless you're in a teaching situation or introducing a new and complex concept, you should use as few visual aids as possible. Select only those aids that clearly enhance the presentation without distracting the audience from paying attention to what you are saying. Backdrop visual aids, such as a company logo or some other image relevant to the occasion, are always appropriate and you should never hesitate to use them.

Visual aids designed to make the speech more entertaining, such as the occasional cartoon or effective picture, are perfectly fine to use. Remember, though, that if you're using someone else's material, such as a comic strip panel or picture, permission must be obtained from the copyright holder and credit given.

The Problem with Visual Aids

You wouldn't be too thrilled if there was a competing event going on while you were speaking. Yet overly produced visual aids, and especially sound and light shows, constitute competing events, right there on the stage with you. You wouldn't want another speaker on the podium talking at the same time as you, would you? Well, sophisticated audiovisuals can be just about the same thing, or maybe worse.

Too much light, sound, and imagery will reduce you to a faceless and forgettable technician. You want the audience to go away talking about you and what you had to say; you don't want them to remember only the great sound and light show.

The reason you're there in person, rather than having just sent a letter, memo, voicemail, or email to the attendees, is the inherent value of having the author of a message physically in front of the intended audience. It is your chance to show how well you know your subject. It is your chance to interact with the audience. Your being there gives the audience the opportunity to get a feel for you as a person. They get to see the expression on your face, observe your body language, and listen to the tone of your voice as your message is being delivered. The overuse of visual aids interferes with all of that. If the audience wanted to watch a video they probably would have done so at home or at the office. They came to see and hear you.

If you rely too much on visual aids the audience will think that you don't have the confidence, ability, or conviction to deliver a powerful speech. The more visual aids you use, the less you come across as a leader, so the more senior and respected you are, the fewer visual aids you should use. The CEO should *never* use visual aids except as a backdrop, such as the company name and logo, or some other image relevant to the occasion. If there is content in the CEO's speech that requires visual aids for clarification, someone else should give that part of the presentation. For example, budget details should be presented by the chief financial officer, not by the chief executive officer.

Another reason to shy away from overly sophisticated audiovisuals is that additional complexity increases the odds of something going wrong. You've probably sat uncomfortably in an audience while the speaker fumbled with the "next" and "back" buttons, or continually interrupted the presentation to instruct another person, who was operating the equipment, to go to the next image, return to the last one, or skip a couple. It's disconcerting to the audience, destroys the flow of the presentation, and diminishes the reputation of the speaker.

Sophisticated, computer-driven technology is extremely useful during preparation, but always confirm to yourself that it will enhance your presentation rather than detract from it. Make sure that you clearly know how to operate the equipment or have a competent person assisting you, and always include the assistant and the technology in your rehearsals.

Visual aids must not be your message; they should just support your message.

Before using a visual aid, make sure that it is:

1. Relevant
2. Informative
3. Necessary
4. Foolproof
5. Worth the trouble and expense.

Content

Visual aids containing only words are usually redundant and rarely add anything to a speech (sometimes slides containing point summaries of what you're saying can be helpful, however). People can read a lot faster than you can talk. If the visual aid just repeats what you're saying, the audience will read what's on the screen rather than listen to and look at you. They will miss your tone of voice, inflection, and body language, all of which may be extremely important to your credibility and to the persuasiveness of your message. Worse still, they will finish the thought before you do; then their minds will wander and you'll completely lose their attention.

Whenever possible it's better to use pictures and graphs rather than words and numbers. Graphs are much more understandable than tables or rows and columns of numbers. A table with complex data confuses, but a simple graph clarifies. Eliminate all clutter. An audience will grasp and remember a clear, graphic presentation but will usually ignore and always quickly forget a complex table.

Unless it's a summary of points that you've covered, deal with just one main point per visual aid. Be sure that the contents of the visual aid can be clearly seen by the entire audience. If you have to read to the audience what's on a visual aid, then the visual aid is worse than useless.

Using Visual Aids

When using a visual aid, explain in advance the point that's going to be illustrated on it, then show the visual aid as evidence to back up, not just repeat, what you said. Talking and showing a visual aid at the same time, unless it's just a summary or a simple backdrop, can be confusing and redundant. Talk, then show, is the way to go.

If the visual aid is not a summary or backdrop, don't let the audience see it until you've introduced what's going to be on it, and then get it out of the way as soon as you've dealt with it.

Never use a visual aid solely for dramatic effect; it must also support or enhance your message. If you're good and if you've prepared properly, you don't need gimmicks. People remember two types of speakers: the best they've heard and the worst they've heard. You'll never make it into the first category if you overuse visual aids.

Don't hand out copies of your visual aids beforehand unless you want them used as a workbook or when introducing a new and complex subject. If the audience has these copies, they will examine them rather than listening to and watching you. They'll no longer be paying attention to the pace, tone, and continuity of your presentation; you'll have lost their attention and a lot of the effectiveness of your talk will have evaporated.

Finally, never speak to the audience while you're turned to look at your visual aid. If you have to look at the visual aid for some reason, stop talking. Always talk to the audience, never to the visual aid.

In a nutshell . . .

1. Unless in a teaching situation or when introducing a new and complex subject, use as few visual aids as possible.

2. Visual aids that make a speech more entertaining, such as a cartoon, and backdrop visuals, such as a company logo, shouldn't be a problem.

3. If you're using copyrighted material, such as a comic strip panel, permission must be obtained and credit given.

4. Visual aids should never dominate a presentation; you want the audience to remember you and your message, not just the sound and light show.

5. The more visual aids you use, the less you come across as a leader.

6. The only visual aids a CEO should use are backdrops or other images relevant to the occasion, never information visuals.

7. Don't get mired in technology.

8. Visual aids should just support your message, not be your message.

9. The criteria for visual aids are that they be relevant, informative, necessary, foolproof, and worth the time and expense.

10. Pictures are better than words, and graphs are better than numbers.

11. Unless it's a summary, deal with just one main point per visual aid.

12. Unless it's a summary or a backdrop, don't let the audience see the visual aid until you've introduced what's going to be on it.

13. When you've finished with the visual aid, get rid of it.

14. Never use a visual aid solely for dramatic effect; it must also support your message.

15. Don't hand out copies of your visual aids beforehand unless you want them used as a workbook.

16. Never talk with your back or side turned to the audience while looking at a visual aid.

REHEARSE, REHEARSE, REHEARSE

In chapter 2, Managing Fear, I expressed puzzlement as to why people who wouldn't for a second expect to be able to play like Oscar Peterson the first time they sit down at a piano, think an audience will expect them to perform like Winston Churchill the first time they speak in front of a group. Of course such expectations exist only in the mind of the rookie speaker. I'm equally puzzled, though, as to why so many speakers, rookies and seasoned veterans alike, think they don't need to rehearse. Everyone needs to rehearse.

A number of years ago I happened to be in the great pop singer Anne Murray's dressing room in Las Vegas just before her final performance of a lengthy engagement. She was rehearsing her hit song "Snowbird," a song she had sung thousands of times, and probably at least ten times that week. Yet she felt that something wasn't quite right with the last rendition, and there she was, with her guitar player, going over it again just before taking the stage. Except in instant, breaking-news situations, professional newscasters always rehearse what they're going to say before going on the air. World-class athletes practice their skills over and over throughout their careers. It's been said that Al MacInnis (no relation to the author), one of the hardest and most accurate shooters in National Hockey League history, used to shoot the puck ten thousand times between seasons. If accomplished superstars like Anne Murray and Al MacInnis and seasoned broadcasters recognize the need to practice what they do regularly for a living, why should you or I ever think that we don't need to practice something that we do only occasionally?

The audience hears what you say only while you're saying it. When you're delivering your speech, the audience doesn't have the time to pause and reflect on your words, nor do they have the opportunity to stop your speech, rewind it, and listen to certain parts of it again. The only way to be sure your content and delivery are appropriate and effective is to rehearse. Rehearsing is the best way to become familiar with your material, and it is the only way to determine how it actually sounds.

Rehearsing allows you to identify and eliminate words that you have difficulty pronouncing and phrases that look fine on paper but turn into tongue twisters at the lectern. Rehearsing lets you determine whether your sentences are too long (it's probably not possible for them to be too short). Rehearsing helps you determine pacing, where pauses will be the most effective, and where added emphasis is required. A great deal of rewriting and improvement of your material will take place during proper rehearsals. The only way to accurately time the length of your speech is to rehearse it.

It's a good idea to rehearse a talk at a lectern (with your visual aids, if any) in front of a few people. Be careful about heeding the advice you receive from members of your practice audience. Unless the person advising you is a skilled speaker, or the advice is obviously sound, rely more on your own instincts about how well the rehearsal went. Be sure that the rehearsal audience understands that you will be stopping frequently to make changes in wording and to try different approaches in your delivery. Do not attempt an uninterrupted run-through, even for timing purposes, until you are completely comfortable with your content.

The ideal way to rehearse a talk would be the same way, but in front of an experienced, skilled speaking coach who will record your rehearsal so that the two of you can view and critique it together. Although you should take a professional coach's advice more seriously than you would that of friends, relatives, and colleagues, remember that the speech is yours and that you alone will be responsible for the effect it will have on the audience. Keep an open mind, but if you're uncomfortable with the expert advice, be sure that the coach has compelling reasons before you accept any suggested changes that don't feel right to you.

You can rehearse by yourself, but try to do so at least once standing at a lectern. Do not rehearse in front of a mirror. You'll spend far too much time and energy looking at yourself rather than concentrating on content and delivery, all the while forgetting that you're actually seeing things backward in any event.

Then there is a lot of effective informal rehearsing that you can do. Simply reading the speech out loud is helpful. You can go over the main points and experiment with different words and phrases in your mind every chance you get, such as when showering, riding in elevators, or waiting in traffic. You can slip parts of the speech into everyday conversations with colleagues, friends, or family members. You can also ask colleagues, friends, and family members to listen to parts of it in order to get their feedback and to judge for yourself how it sounds.

It is not possible to over-rehearse. The more you rehearse, either formally or informally, the more comfortable and confident you will be when you stand at the lectern and say, "Good evening, ladies and gentlemen, it's a great pleasure to be here," rather than, "Unaccustomed as I am to public speaking. . . ."

In a nutshell . . .

1. All talks need to be rehearsed.
2. Professionals in all walks of life continuously practice their craft, so why shouldn't you practice something you do only occasionally?
3. Rehearsing allows you to eliminate words you have difficulty pronouncing.
4. Rehearsing will alert you to difficult or cumbersome phrasing.
5. The only way to know how a speech actually sounds is to rehearse it out loud.
6. Rehearsing is the only way to accurately time your presentation.
7. Rehearse at least once at a lectern, with your visual aids, if any.
8. Don't attempt an uninterrupted run-through, even for timing purposes, until you're completely comfortable with your content.
9. Rehearsing in front of a mirror is useless and possibly harmful.

→

→

10. There are lots of opportunities to informally rehearse the talk in your mind.

11. Look for opportunities to rehearse parts of your talk during normal conversations.

12. Try out parts of your speech on colleagues, friends, or family members.

13. It's not possible to over-rehearse.

Chapter 8

DELIVERY

Your reputation or your topic might entice bodies into the seats, but it will take an effective speech to keep their minds in the room. Even if you've written the best speech ever, all can be lost at the delivery stage.

Get There Early

You should arrive at the venue at least a half hour before the time you're scheduled to speak. If there are speakers scheduled before you, do your best to arrive a half hour before they start to speak. It's always to your advantage to hear what the speakers preceding you have to say.

Look for potential logistical problems and have them fixed before you are to begin, such as:

1. The height and size of the lectern. It should be wide enough to accommodate two sheets of paper side by side, high enough that you can easily see your notes, and low enough for you to comfortably see over and be seen by the audience.

2. Whether microphones are working. (There are few things as amateurish as a speaker tapping a microphone upon arriving at the lectern and asking if it's working.)

3. The availability of drinking water. (To minimize spills, never have your glass more than half full.)

4. Whether there are background noises that need to be eliminated

5. Whether there are any lights that will distract you.

Ask your host whether the makeup of your audience is pretty much the same as was expected when you first discussed the event. If the audience is slightly different than earlier anticipated, there shouldn't be any problems. But if it's dramatically different, for example much older or younger, you may have to do some last-minute editing of your content.

You should determine how many people are expected, and ask the organizers to get rid of unneeded chairs in the back rows. People tend to sit at the back of a room and empty chairs up front make a bad impression.

Don't stand off in a corner with the host or by yourself. Circulate and introduce yourself to some members of the audience. Try to find out some things about them. Learn the names of a few to use, if appropriate and in context, when delivering your speech. If you're going to mention a name or two, be sure to get the pronunciation right. Jot down the names on your script or on a separate card and, unless it's a one-syllable name, spell it out phonetically.

When the Event Begins

Once the event begins, listen carefully to everything that's said before you speak. What goes on before you arrive at the lectern can often provide sources of humor, spontaneity, and immediacy. The audience will also be impressed that you've been paying attention to what's going on around you. They will interpret this as a strong indication that you're a confident, well-prepared person who's probably worth listening to. Listening carefully can also keep you out of trouble; for example, you might learn that the sponsoring organization's president just received a significant award and you can add your congratulations.

Be watchful for incompetent organizers, chairpersons, and introducers. Even if you've followed the advice in chapter 3, What, Where, When, and to Whom, about providing information to them, they'll often get your qualifications wrong or may invent information to make you sound more important than you really are; exaggeration can be worse than understatement.

Even while listening carefully to the proceedings before you speak, it's a good idea to scan the audience from time to time in order to gain a degree of familiarity with them and to gauge their reactions to what's going on.

Your Opening

If the audience hasn't had a break in the hour before you begin to speak, you should relinquish a moment or two of your time to give them a chance to stretch their legs. This will not only make you very popular with the audience, but will also allow you more time to become comfortable with your surroundings.

If you're not going to have a leg stretch, take a few seconds to get a good look around the audience before you start. Audiences don't mind watching you give them the once-over; it's a sign that you're thinking on your feet and that you're in control.

Thank your introducer but don't restate any of your qualifications; at this point it would just sound pompous. However, if the introducer made errors in the introduction that absolutely need to be corrected, such as announcing the wrong topic, identifying you with the wrong company, or grossly overstating your qualifications, now is the time to good-naturedly set the record straight.

Don't start off with apologies, unless you were late arriving. Everything else can be ignored. For example, if you have a slight cold don't call attention to it by apologizing (unless, of course, you sneeze). A cold that's bad enough to warrant an apology is probably bad enough to warrant a cancellation.

As mentioned in chapter 3, being at the venue early enough to hear any preceding speakers may pay off as you open your talk. If one of them said something relevant to your talk, mention it here. The audience will see that you cared enough to be there early, were paying attention to the earlier speakers, and are confident enough in your own ability as a speaker not to be afraid to refer to what someone else had to say.

The Four Forces

You have four forces at work during your delivery:

1. Your words
2. Your voice

3. Your face (particularly your eyes)

4. Your body.

They must all work together to convey a consistent message. Try looking in the mirror and saying "I love you" with a hateful, angry look on your face and you'll get an idea of what I mean. Or look in the mirror and say the following with a two-second pause between each word: "I . . . am . . . really . . . excited."

Tone of voice, facial expressions, and body language are as important as your actual words. Indeed, sometimes audiences will react more to your nonverbal signals than to your words. If your facial expression and body language don't reflect your words, the audience may be thinking, "He's saying it's a pleasure to be talking to us, but he doesn't really feel that way." They'll think that you're either not comfortable with your material or that you're a hypocrite; they may even think both.

When your words, facial expressions, tone of voice, and body language are not consistent, the audience receives a confusing and ineffective series of signals. Your believability suffers the most. We dealt with your words during the preparation stage, so here we'll discuss the other three forces: voice, face, and body.

YOUR VOICE

The secret to looking and sounding natural and confident is to be conversational. This means speaking with the same pace, timing, pauses, inflection, and emphasis that you would use in an animated conversation with a bunch of friends around the dinner table. A good speech is just good, effective conversation standing up rather than sitting down.

Never slip into a monotone. Always be sure to emphasize what needs to be emphasized. To understand the importance of this point, repeat the following sentence six times, emphasizing a different word each time: I never said he stole money. The same six words will have six different meanings.

If you have a microphone, you don't need to speak more loudly than normal. If you have to speak more loudly than normal in order to be audible to everyone in the room, then you should have a microphone.

YOUR FACE

If you want the people in the audience to enjoy themselves, you have to look like *you're* enjoying yourself; you can't do that with scowls and frowns. Scowls and frowns never go over well with audiences. Smile, but not like a grinning idiot. Natural smiles, at the right places, are the smiles that work. Never stifle a smile or a chuckle unless it's a smile or a chuckle at someone else's expense.

As with your tone of voice, try to use the same facial expressions you would if you were in conversation with a few good friends. Have a good time or the audience won't; an audience that's having a good time is far easier to persuade than one that's uncomfortable, bored, or antagonistic.

You've got to let your audience know that you care about them. One of the best ways to do this is to make eye contact with people throughout your presentation. You should pick out a person and look right at him or her for a couple of seconds and then move on to another person in another part of the room. Be sure to include all areas of the room, but don't get into a fixed pattern, such as left-front, left-back, right-back, right-front. Keep them guessing as to who will be your next target. This not only makes your eye contact more natural and effective but, because they don't know whom you're going to look at next, it helps you to keep the entire audience's attention.

You should never let the house lights be dimmed to the point where you can't see and make eye contact with your audience. If this means eliminating your visual aids, then eliminate them. If you want your audience to pay attention to you, then you must pay attention to your audience.

BODY LANGUAGE

When it's your turn to speak, approach the lectern confidently with your head held high and your shoulders back. When you get to the lectern, stand erect. Don't slump. Don't tense your shoulders. Don't sway. Don't rock. If you have any of these bad habits, work hard to break them.

It's always better to stand than to sit, even in small groups and informal surroundings. Standing sends a message of energy, enthusiasm, confidence, and control.

If the circumstances warrant it, for example when you're speaking off the cuff with a portable microphone, or to a relatively small audience, it's perfectly all right to move around the stage, but don't pace around like a caged animal; this can be very distracting to an audience. If you're going to move around, be sure you don't get into a set pattern that the audience will begin monitoring instead of paying attention to what you're saying. Stay at the lectern if you want to play it completely safe.

GESTURES

The problem with gestures is not that people don't know how to effectively use their hands and arms; the problem is that when people get in front of an audience, they tend to do things that prevent them from gesturing spontaneously and naturally.

Perhaps the most egregious thing that speakers do is rattling coins in a pocket. Do this and in no time the audience will be thinking, "That's a dime or two, perhaps a nickel, a couple of quarters . . ." instead of paying attention to what you're saying. If you have this habit, be sure your pockets are empty when addressing a group. In extreme cases, if you still can't keep your hands out of your pockets, with or without coins, you may have to sew them up when making a talk.

Another gesture-destroying move is locking your hands behind your back; still another is to grip the lectern as if you, or it, are in danger of flying away.

Some speakers tap the lectern or their notes with a pen or their fingers. These idiosyncrasies annoy an audience at the best of times, and will drive them to distraction if the microphone is particularly sensitive. If you do these things, stop.

Here's the best way to break these habits. When you're starting to speak, or if you catch yourself falling into a bad habit during your presentation, rest your fingertips lightly on the lectern and then forget about them. Your normal habits will take over and your gestures will become natural, spontaneous, and completely appropriate.

If you just forget about what your hands and arms are doing, they'll do just fine by themselves. Nearly everyone gestures naturally while conversing at a party with friends, and it need be no different in front of a group. Just let your arms and hands do what comes naturally.

Interaction with the Audience

Audience participation is always effective, so if there's an appropriate, nondisruptive way to engage them, don't hesitate to do so. You can have audience participation with large groups simply by asking rhetorical questions or by asking for a show of hands. Anything that gets an audience thinking along with you is beneficial in building a rapport with them.

Rhetorical questions are designed to get the audience thinking about the issue while you go on to develop the answer during your presentation. An example of a rhetorical question is, "What if we all stopped paying our income tax?"

If you want the audience to respond to a question by a show of hands, tell them that you expect them to do so. Say something like, "I'm wondering how many of you feel that you have enough insurance; if you do, please raise your hand." And, of course, always take the time to look around and get a feel for the response.

But never make fools of an audience. I once saw a speaker think he was getting effective audience participation by asking everyone to turn around and shake hands with the person behind them. Of course, this is impossible because everyone is then turned around. All he succeeded in doing was insult the audience. You always have to respect your audience. If you don't, they'll sense it and nothing you say or do will please them.

A delicate type of audience interaction arises when someone begins to heckle you. It's very difficult to generalize about heckling situations, but you will rarely come out ahead by getting into a mudslinging match. The rest of the audience will usually start out on your side, but if you argue with the heckler your support will soon start to splinter. Be firm and courteous, but keep control of the situation. Being diplomatic will count more than being quick or clever, so maintain your composure. As the adage advises, you should always engage brain before starting tongue. A good technique is to suggest to the heckler that you'll be happy to discuss matters one-on-one after your presentation. Then ignore him. If this doesn't work, you may have to resort to asking whoever is in charge of the event to have the person cautioned or, in an extreme case, removed.

After an interruption such as a heckler, you have to regain your audience's attention without creating a feeling of hostility or confrontation. Don't refer to the incident other than to apologize for the disturbance, then briefly summarize where you were in your talk and get on with your presentation. Resist letting your mind wander back to whatever happened; concentrate instead on delivering your message and finishing your talk in a positive vein.

If someone in the audience corrects a mistake you've made, admit you were wrong, thank them, and move on. Never get caught being purposefully evasive. When someone agrees with a point you've made, just say, "Thank you" and let it go at that. Always! Otherwise you may seem like members of some mutual admiration society, or the questioner may look like a plant. In either case, your credibility suffers.

Enthusiasm and Emotion

Remember that it's perfectly fine to let your emotions shine through. Good speakers bring personality, excitement, and passion to what they're saying. Audiences are interested in you as a person, so don't be afraid to show them your heart as well as your face.

Emotion is a two-sided communication coin. Positive, genuine emotions are constructive persuasive forces, but negative or insincere emotions create barriers. Use your emotions to your advantage. Being cold, aloof, or ill-tempered will never make you well liked. If you behave like you don't believe in your message, no one else will believe in it either. On the other hand, being enthusiastic and upbeat will win people over.

Audiences appreciate and respect speakers who clearly believe in what they are saying. The audience may disagree with you, but they are less likely to become hostile if they believe in your sincerity. If you consistently demonstrate to the audience that you feel strongly about what you're saying, you can pretty well stop worrying about any other speaking technique. Communicate your convictions by saying what you know and showing how you feel.

Inexperienced speakers tend to be too inhibited or too over-the-top. Just be yourself. You don't have to dramatically change your personality or become a phony. Nobody can be you as well as you can.

The audience needs to know that you care. If you don't care enough about your subject, change the topic or cancel the speech.

Pace

Use appropriate pacing, pauses, and timing to make the best impact. Don't speak too fast (though you do need to pick up your pace for teenagers and children, who have shorter attention spans). Pauses are essential and effective parts of any speech. In addition to providing emphasis, pauses allow an audience to catch up with you while you catch your breath. Wonderful places for pauses are right after a rhetorical question or when you've lost your place.

Remember, though, there's a difference between a pause and a silence. Pauses should never be more than a few seconds.

Never talk over applause or laughter, always wait them out.

When time is short, don't talk faster, talk less. Edit as you go along. End with conviction and never introduce new material near the end of your talk.

Word Whiskers and Trite Phrases

Word whiskers are expressions such as "er," "um," and "ah"; the ungrammatical use of the phrase "you know" and the word "like"; and ending sentences with "okay?" All of these verbal tics imply that you either don't know your material very well or that you are an inarticulate person, neither of which is a very favorable portrayal.

Trite phrases may have been meaningful at one time, or in a particular context, but through overuse, they have become meaningless. They tend to be used by speakers who are too lazy to search for accurate, descriptive words or phrases. Hackneyed phrases are always boring; they also cheat the audience out of a clear explanation of your message.

Examples of trite phrases currently popular with business executives and professionals include:

1. At the end of the day

2. Going forward

3. Best practices

4. Value added

5. Ramp up

6. Tone at the top

7. Thinking outside the box

8. Tipping point

9. In terms of

10. Ahead of (or behind) the curve.

If you're prone to using word whiskers and trite phrases, you need to break the habit. Ask family members, friends, and colleagues to point out when your message needs a shave or is becoming lazy. Getting rid of word whiskers and trite phrases will not just make you a better public speaker; it will also make you a better everyday conversationalist.

Never Run Overtime

If there is a set time for adjournment, end before that time, even if the master of ceremonies has told you that it's okay to run a bit late.

If the program has gotten behind schedule, make as many points as you can, express your regret for the fact that you don't have enough time to deliver your whole speech, and sit down. There's nothing for you to gain by compounding the lateness of the overall program.

Don't tell the audience how much longer you're going to speak or how much material you have left to deliver. You may not be able to live up to the promise, and you can be sure that the audience will be holding you to it. Above all, never keep talking when you have nothing more to say.

Don't Hand Out Copies Beforehand

Except as explained below under Reading a Speech, you should not hand out copies of your speech until you've finished speaking. There are three reasons for this:

1. As mentioned in chapter 6, Visual Aids, people can read a great deal faster than you can talk. If they have a copy of your presentation, they'll likely read it ahead of your speaking it.

2. If the audience has copies of your speech, you will be disinclined to depart from the written version, thereby eliminating the possibility of spontaneity or instant editing, both of which are potential advantages that you should not relinquish.

3. Your presentation should have been written to be heard, not read. The audience can't get the true meaning of your words simply by reading them. The words need to be heard in conjunction with your inflection, timing, emphasis, pauses, facial expressions, body language, and gestures.

Reading a Speech

There are only two situations in which you should read your speech verbatim. One is when your lawyer insists upon it. The other is when you are getting TV or radio coverage and the producers have picked out the part they want to record, so you need to stick to the script. In this latter situation, it's okay to give the production crew a copy of your speech but you should still not allow the general audience to have copies for the three reasons outlined above.

Here are the rules for reading a speech:

1. Make sure the script is typed as outlined in chapter 5, Writing the Speech.

2. Mark up the script with cues for pauses, pacing, and word emphasis.

3. Pause after every key point.

4. Pause after every sentence.

5. Constantly make eye contact with your audience.

6. Don't use a teleprompter until you've mastered its use through rehearsal.

Appearance

Be well-groomed and dress just a little bit better than the occasion calls for. Always make sure that you feel comfortable (both physically and mentally) in what you're wearing. Err on the side of conservatism, but remember that audiences tend to accept speakers who look and dress much like they expected that they would.

If you need glasses, wear them, but be sure they fit properly. Constantly having to push up your glasses is annoying and distracting for both you and the audience. Jewelry can be distracting and noisy, it often reflects light, and it can be cumbersome. You certainly don't want to wear a bracelet that could hook onto your notes and spill them onto the floor.

This is a good time to mention that you should not take off your watch and place it on the lectern in front of you. Many speakers think this sends the message that they care about finishing on time, but it actually indicates that the speaker is unprepared, unrehearsed, and has no idea how long the speech is.

Style

I'm often asked by people, especially senior executives and professionals, what their delivery "style" should be. The answer is "just be yourself." Many executives are trained to think that they have to conform to some model of perfection. That's inconsistent with being a good public speaker and usually results in dull, uninspiring presentations. If executives tried as hard to be human and ordinary as they do to be perfect, they'd be much more effective speakers. An audience will always prefer an imperfect but interesting speaker to a technically perfect bore.

But there is always some fine-tuning that can be applied to your speaking style. Ways you can improve your style have been mentioned elsewhere in this book; they include:

1. Getting rid of annoying habits, such as using word whiskers and trite phrases

2. Allowing yourself to gesture naturally

3. Speaking in a conversational tone

4. Using timing, your tone of voice, and inflection for emphasis and variety

5. Not being afraid to let your feelings show.

As important as fine-tuning is, it's equally important that you don't try to develop different styles for different situations. Be consistently yourself, at your very best, in every situation. Be the same person whether you're giving a speech, engaging in a conversation, or being interviewed by the media. Don't change your innate style just because the situation changes. An exception, of course, is that you may have to be a little more or a little less formal depending on the situation. For example, luncheon presentations tend to be relatively informal, whereas corporate annual meetings are usually highly structured, formal events.

Except to get the adrenaline flowing—a goal that should be the exception rather than the rule (see chapter 1, The Right Topic)—you shouldn't need to become an actor to effectively communicate your ideas, but you do need to perform. In this context, there's quite a difference between acting and performing. Acting is being someone other than who you really are; performing is being yourself at your absolute best.

One style every speaker should aspire to is being likeable. Here are some rules you should never break:

1. Don't whine and complain.

2. Don't dwell on trivialities.

3. Don't be self-centered.

4. Don't talk down to people.

5. Don't try to please everybody; you'll likely end up pleasing no one.

6. Do become sincerely interested in other people.

7. Do be optimistic.

8. Do laugh easily, especially at yourself. If you goof, own up to it and continue on your way; the audience will love you for it.

If the audience likes you, they'll forgive almost anything you do wrong. If they don't like you, you've got a tough row to hoe no matter how well prepared and technically perfect you may be.

In a nutshell . . .

1. Arrive at the venue early, check it out carefully, and have any problems taken care of.

2. Determine if the audience will be of the size and makeup you anticipated. If not, consider whether you have to do some last-minute editing.

3. When the event begins, pay attention to everything that goes on, especially your introduction.

4. If the audience hasn't had a break in the hour before you begin to speak, give them a short leg-stretch.

5. It's fine to mention the names of a couple of people in the audience, but be sure you get the pronunciation correct.

6. Tone of voice, facial expressions, and body language are as important as your actual words.

7. Use inflection, word emphasis, timing, and pauses, but do so in a conversational tone, just as you would when telling a story to a group of friends.

8. Smiles, if they're real, are good; chuckles are great, as long as they're not at someone else's expense.

9. Make continual eye contact with all parts of the audience, but don't get into a set pattern.

10. Stand erect, don't slump, don't tense your shoulders, don't rock or sway; look like someone who's worth listening to.

11. Don't hold on to the lectern, put your hands in your pockets or clasp them behind your back, or otherwise prevent your gestures from coming naturally.

12. To ensure natural gestures, lightly rest your fingertips on the lectern and forget about them; your arms and hands will then do just fine on their own.

13. Audience participation is always effective—even if it's just through rhetorical questions or a show of hands.

14. Never, ever, insult your audience.

15. Deal with hecklers diplomatically, but deal with them.

16. Don't worry about letting your feelings show.

17. Don't talk too fast.

18. If you're running out of time, talk less not faster; never run overtime.

19. Except in extraordinary circumstances, don't read a speech or hand out copies beforehand.

20. Dress just a little better than the occasion calls for.

21. If you need glasses, wear them, but be sure they fit.

22. Be yourself, but be yourself at your very best.

QUESTION AND ANSWER PERIODS

There are two types of question and answer periods that you might encounter as a speaker: the audience question and answer period and the press conference. Because the general audience tends to defer too much to them, if there are media people in attendance, you should arrange to deal with them separately. This chapter addresses the general audience question and answer period; dealing with the media is covered in chapter 10.

Beyond the fact that you should not allow questions during or after a formal dinner speech (refer to chapter 4, Before You Begin to Write the Speech), there are a few other decisions that you and the organizers should make based on your particular circumstances: whether you're going to have a formal question and answer period after you've finished speaking, whether you're going to allow questions during your presentation, or whether you're not going to entertain questions at all. The chosen format is not as important as making sure that the decision is made before you start your presentation, that the audience is clearly informed at the outset what the rules for questions are, and that you and the organizers stick to the rules.

For presentations that are less than an hour long, it's usually best not to allow questions during the talk, but rather to hold them until the end. On the other hand, during long presentations you shouldn't force the audience to sit on their questions for more than an hour.

Allowing questions from the floor during short presentations interrupts your pacing and flow, and if the audience has a lot of questions you will have to cut them off or run late. You never want to run overtime and cutting off questioners can be seen as rude, whereas ending a post-presentation question and answer period when the allotted time is up is usually accepted in good grace, particularly if you offer to stay around and answer individual questions.

For presentations over an hour you should break at a convenient place for questions rather than leave them until you're finished speaking. But still have a defined time limit and do not exceed it lest you put yourself in a position of having to cut out material or run late, neither of which is desirable.

The audience should be informed of the question period time limits and what the rules are, such as whether they have to identify themselves or go to strategically placed microphones to voice their queries. For large audiences, 100 to 200 people, microphones are a great advantage. For very large audiences, more than 200 people, microphones are absolutely essential, and you might also want to allow written questions.

If written questions are to be used, paper and pencils must be provided to everyone and there should be enough people assigned to pick up the questions and bring them to the podium in a timely fashion. Audiences often appreciate written questions, since they can jot down their thoughts while you're still speaking. Written questions can be helpful to you since you can choose the order in which you deal with them and even exclude particular questions if you wish.

It's better to have the master of ceremonies inform the audience what the question and answer format and rules are going to be than for you to have to do it during your opening. But if no such announcement has been made, you should do it.

Be extremely alert during the question and answer period. It's a tremendous opportunity to redeem yourself in areas where your talk may not have gone as well as you wanted, and to enhance your performance in areas where it did.

Listen attentively to what the question ultimately is, rather than anticipating what it's going to be. It's dangerous to start formulating your answer halfway through the question. You may completely miss a change of direction at the end of the question with the result that your answer will sound evasive, deceitful, or just plain stupid.

Many experienced speakers will save some new material for the question and answer period. If the appropriate question doesn't get asked, they'll generate it themselves in the form of a rhetorical question or prefaced by a comment such as, "Some of you may have been wondering. . . ."

It's always a good idea to ensure that there will be a couple of good questions to start the ball rolling. The best way to accomplish this is to plant a couple of questions in the audience. If you haven't arranged this beforehand, start off by asking, "Who has the first question?" If no one responds you can usually kick-start it by saying, "A question I'm often asked is. . . ."

If you get a question that's based on an incorrect premise, set the record straight before you respond. For example, after I'd given a talk during which I'd speculated on what income tax changes the government might be introducing, a member of the audience began his question, "You obviously have some inside connections in government. . . ." Before answering the actual question, I made it clear that my answer was based strictly on my own expectations and not based on actual knowledge, inside or otherwise.

A short and incisive question always deserves a short and incisive answer; so does a long, drawn-out question. Don't get into long, convoluted answers. You've already given your speech, don't start giving another one at this point. In handling a long-winded question, concisely restate the question in your own words before answering. Everyone will then know what you're talking about and you'll be able to give an appropriate answer. You should also repeat any question that everyone in the audience wasn't able to hear.

Don't answer too quickly. If you need a little time to think about your answer, take it. Making sure that you really know what you're about to say helps you get rid of word whiskers and trite phrases and eliminate redundancies. The audience will see you as a thoughtful person who's not shooting from the hip, or the lip, as the case might be. If you pause slightly before all your answers, it won't seem like you're panicking when the really tough question that requires extra thought comes along. However, once you begin your answer, get right to the point. Giving illustrations and examples to back up your answers is always appreciated by the audience and tends to keep your answers crisp and to the point.

In informal situations, such as a presentation to your staff or fellow club members, you can be more conversational and indulge in more give-and-take with the audience than would be acceptable in a larger, more formal setting.

Deal with belligerent questioners the same way you would a heckler during your main presentation. Separate how you feel about the questioner from the subject being discussed. Watch your tone of voice, stay cool, stay sincere, stay likeable, and never embarrass a questioner, regardless of how tempting or justified it may seem. But don't turn into a wimp. When someone disagrees with your point of view, stay true to yourself. Give your answer as an opinion if you wish, but don't back off further than that. To defuse loaded questions don't hesitate to question the questioner. Asking belligerent questioners why they feel the way they do, or on what information their opinion is based, is often all that's needed to get things back on track.

As is the case during the delivery of your speech, if a questioner points out a mistake you've made or simply agrees with you, just thank the person and move on.

Never try to fake it. If you don't know the answer to a question, say so. If at all possible refer the questioner to a source where the answer may be found. If practical, you can offer to meet the questioner after your session is over and obtain a telephone number, fax number, or email address to which you can forward the answer once you've had time to research it.

End the question and answer period when the audience has obviously run out of interesting questions or at the scheduled ending time, whichever occurs first. Never run overtime, but if there are clearly more people with questions, offer to stay around for a while to deal with them.

In a nutshell . . .

1. Don't deal with the media during the general audience question and answer period; arrange a separate press conference.

2. Be sure the format for questions and answers is made clear to the audience and stick to the rules as agreed upon between you and the organizers.

3. It's usually best not to allow questions during a presentation that is less than an hour long; leave them until the end.

4. For presentations longer than an hour, break for questions.

5. It's usually a good idea to offer to stay around and answer individual questions after the event.

6. Be prepared to kick-start the question and answer period in case the audience is slow to get involved.

7. If you get a question that's based on an incorrect premise, set the record straight before you answer.

8. Keep answers as short and incisive as possible.

9. Don't answer too quickly; if you need a little time to think, take it.

10. Illustrations and examples are extremely useful for keeping your answers on point.

11. Restate confusing questions so that the audience can understand them.

12. Repeat questions that everyone in the audience wasn't able to hear.

→

→

13. Deal with belligerent questioners the same way you would deal with a heckler: politely but firmly.

14. When a questioner rightly points out a mistake you've made, acknowledge it, thank the person, and move on.

15. When someone simply agrees with something you've said, just say thank you and move on.

16. Never try to fake it; if you don't know the answer to a question, say so.

17. End the question and answer period when the audience runs out of interesting questions or when the time is up, whichever happens first.

DEALING WITH THE MEDIA

The advice given in the previous chapter largely applies to dealing with the media as well; the most important point is to be yourself. Just as you shouldn't try to be different people to different audiences, you shouldn't change your personal style for different media. Whether you're dealing with radio, television, or print, be yourself.

When working with the media, you have to be an extremely conscientious listener. Whether in a press conference or a one-on-one interview, you simply have to give your undivided attention to what the journalist is asking. Just as in a general audience question and answer period, you should never start formulating your answer until you've heard the entire question and understand exactly what it's about.

Remember the particular hat that you're wearing on the occasion of your interaction with the media. Questions don't always have a context, but you can be sure that your answer will at least have a perceived context. For example, you can more credibly get into a discussion on the dreadful condition of the city streets when speaking as the chair of a ratepayers' group than you could when speaking as the CEO of a street paving firm.

It's also necessary to consider that when you're being interviewed by the media you are, in effect, speaking to many thousands of people with varied views and interests. You have to modify your message accordingly.

"No comment" is not a substitute for "I don't know," and should only be used when you can give a plausible explanation for doing so, such as on advice from your lawyer. Never say "no comment" and let it go at that. If the real answer is that you don't know, then admit it. If you shouldn't be expected to have the requested information, say so and explain why.

The more inflammatory the question, the shorter your answer should be. Don't get both feet in your mouth by giving rambling answers. You're apt to sound like you're protesting too much, or you might say something totally inappropriate. However, simple yes and no answers tend to be viewed as evasive and impolite. Say what you need to say and then shut up. Silence is never your problem; it's the journalist's job to come up with the next question, not yours. If you're being interviewed for a radio or television show, remember that recorded interviews can always be edited, so short answers are less likely to be omitted or misrepresented.

Be likeable, brief, honest, and positive. If you come across as an arrogant ass, the whole purpose of the press conference or the interview may be destroyed. If you're dishonest, you will be caught out, if not right away, then certainly later. Being positive pays off; nobody likes to watch and listen to negative people.

Although you will know more about your subject than the interviewer does in just about every media situation, never adopt a superior attitude. A good journalist will have done a lot of homework and will have access to an amount of research that might astound you; acting like you know more than they do may set you up for a hard fall.

Another thing to remember is that the journalist's views, and perhaps those of the public, may differ from yours. Journalists often have strong opinions, and you will rarely win an argument with a person who owns the microphone. However, just as in a normal question and answer period, if you get a question that's based on an incorrect premise, always, without exception, set the record straight before you respond.

Some questions may contain loaded words or phrases. Don't legitimize such comments by repeating them in your answer. Rephrase them into factual terms. For example, if a journalist says your organization is "irresponsible and a blight on your industry," don't say, "We are not irresponsible and a blight on our industry." Instead, say something like "We're taking the following actions to . . ." and go on to explain your position in a positive light. Sometimes you'll have to point out that the question was loaded by saying something like, "Well, you obviously disagree with us on this, but here are the real facts." Then go into your positive reply.

Don't be rushed into poorly considered or incomplete answers because the journalist has a deadline. That's the journalist's problem, not yours. Keep in mind that you cannot adequately deal with a complicated issue in a seven-second sound bite. The journalist's mission, in part, is to get information to which he or she is not necessarily entitled. The journalist has nothing to lose by interviewing you, but you, and those you represent, could lose a lot by what you say or how you say it.

Many people have gotten into trouble by making off-the-cuff comments that ended up being recorded without their knowledge.

Whenever you are around media people you should always assume the microphones are live, the cameras are running, and notes are being taken, even if it looks like they aren't.

Many people are familiar with the concept of talking with a journalist "off the record." It's not wise to rely on your comments being off the record unless the journalist has explicitly agreed in advance to keep all or part of your remarks off the record, and you are completely confident that he or she will honor the agreement.

In a nutshell . . .

1. Most of the advice given in chapter 9, Question and Answer Periods, applies when dealing with the media, but the following points are also important.

2. Don't set out to be something you're not; just be yourself.

3. Give your undivided attention to the person asking the question; don't anticipate.

4. Remember which hat you're wearing—that is, in what context you're making your remarks.

5. "No comment" is not a substitute for "I don't know" and should never be used without giving a plausible explanation for being unable to comment.

6. If you don't know the answer, say so.

7. Avoid rambling answers, but remember that yes and no answers are usually seen as being evasive and impolite.

8. Remember that recorded interviews can always be edited; short answers are less likely to be omitted or misrepresented.

9. Be likeable, brief, honest, and positive.

10. Always set the record straight when confronted with an incorrect premise.

11. Don't legitimize loaded words or phrases by repeating them.

12. Don't be rushed into poorly considered or incomplete answers.

13. Always assume an open mike, a running camera, and that notes are being taken.

14. The concept of "off the record" should only be relied upon when you completely trust the journalist.

IMPROMPTU SPEAKING

If you're like most people, there are few utterances that strike more fear into your heart than to be sitting in an audience and suddenly realize that the master of ceremonies' sentence that began with, "And now a few words from . . ." actually ended with your name. The prospect of impromptu presentations often paralyzes even the seasoned speaker. It shouldn't. As a matter of fact, you shouldn't at all mind having to make a few unplanned remarks. Hearken back to chapter 1, The Right Topic, and you will realize that all the necessary elements for a successful talk are present in an impromptu speaking situation.

Think for a moment about the settings in which you're likely to be unexpectedly asked to say a few words. The most common of these situations are those in which you have some personal experiences you can draw on, such as weddings and retirement parties. The next most common is when you're attending a meeting. You'd hardly be at the meeting if you had no interest in the topic being discussed. As a matter of fact, you probably have a keen interest in the subject. Accordingly, you are clearly knowledgeable enough to be able to say a few words.

But, what about the other two criteria for a can't-fail talk: caring about the subject and wanting to talk about it? You probably do have feelings about the topic (a friend being married, a colleague being honored, or a point on which you have strong views). As for wanting to talk about it, in any impromptu speaking situation you'll probably gladly have something to say; even if you don't, it should be pretty easy for you to rationalize wanting to. You wouldn't want to disappoint a friend or coworker, and you shouldn't want to pass up an opportunity to make your views known to your colleagues about a subject you care about.

There are two other reasons why you should never be too upset about having to make a few impromptu remarks: first, masters of ceremonies really mean it when they say "a few words"; second, the audience's expectations in these circumstances aren't too high. So, you really have to speak for no more than a minute or two, and you can succeed nicely by telling a story about the friend who's getting married or retiring. At a meeting, making one point backed up with a couple of examples as to why you feel this way will do nicely.

But what do you do when hearing your name called paralyzes your brain? There are two effective methods for gracefully handling this situation; one will work almost all the time and the other will work all the time. You may forget about or neglect the foolproof method and will have to fall back on the almost foolproof one. We'll deal with the latter first.

Remember that in any impromptu speaking situation you will have enough knowledge of the topic to enable you to say something;

you will very likely care in some way about the subject; and you can easily rationalize wanting to say a few words. So, all the elements for a successful talk are there.

You will always have a few moments to organize your thoughts, first by stalling a bit with the "who me?" reaction. You can create even more thinking time by slowly making your way to the podium or the front of the room, and you can always pause for few more seconds when you get there.

During this time ask yourself, "What can I say about this person or topic?" Usually expanding on the first thought that comes into your mind is all you need to do. If it's a person (the wedding or retirement party), you'll probably think of something that happened to at least two people in the room. Just tell that story by answering the classic journalistic questions: What happened? Who was involved? Why did it happen? When did it happen? Where did it happen? How did it happen?

If it's a meeting, make a single point that reveals your views and back it up with an example or two, which can also take the form of a story. As mentioned earlier, you must have some interest or views on the subject or you wouldn't be at the meeting. You can buy some time, if necessary, by asking a clarifying question or two.

Now to the foolproof method, which is quite simple but requires a little bit of work, which is the reason most people don't use it. Anytime you're going to be in a situation where there is the possibility of being asked to say a few words, decide beforehand what you would say should the occasion arise.

For example, if you're going to a wedding reception or a retirement party, go over in your mind what story or stories you will tell if asked to speak. If you're going to a meeting, look over the agenda and clarify your thoughts on each item, specifically what points you'd make if the opportunity arose. Although it's perfectly all right to jot down a few notes, don't refer to them when speaking. This would spoil the spontaneity of the occasion, raise the audience's expectations, and very likely reduce their appreciation of your ability to think on your feet.

In a nutshell . . .

1. Being unexpectedly asked to say a few words can happen anytime you're in a group of people, but rarely when you aren't perfectly qualified and prepared to comply.

2. "A few words" is literally all that's wanted from you, so you only have to speak for a minute or two to fulfill your obligation.

3. The expectations of the audience in these circumstances aren't very high, so there isn't a lot of pressure on you.

4. All impromptu speaking requirements can be met by telling a story or making a single point. Just ask yourself, "What can I say about this person or this topic?" and then expand on the first thing that comes to mind.

5. Anytime you're going to be in a situation where there's even the remotest chance of having to say a few words, give some thought to what you will say if asked.

INTRODUCING AND THANKING A SPEAKER

Although most of the advice contained elsewhere in this book equally applies, this chapter deals with some additional points that need to be considered when introducing or thanking a speaker.

Introducing a Speaker

Even though it should be easy to prepare and deliver, the speech of introduction is probably the most consistently butchered performance known to the human race. There are two reasons for this: first, that people don't understand the purpose of an introduction; and second, that most people underestimate its importance and do not properly prepare for it.

Let's start with why a speech of introduction is necessary. Most introducers think their job is to entertain the audience or to make a speech of their own. Such is not the case. The audience didn't come to hear the introducer; they came to hear the featured speaker.

The introducer's job is to:

1. Remind the audience why the topic is important to them.

2. Establish the speaker's qualifications to speak on the topic.

3. Start the presentation off on a high note by establishing an upbeat tone.

4. Make the speaker feel especially welcome.

All of this can be accomplished in no more than a couple of minutes. If you're slated to be an introducer, get in touch with the speaker well before the day of the event. First, be sure that you have the exact title of the talk. Next, along with the speaker, decide which of the speaker's resume items will convince the audience that the speaker is qualified to speak on the particular topic. You and the speaker should also determine if there are any other points of interest about the speaker that should be included in the introduction. Then you need to develop a reason or two why this speech will be important to this particular audience.

Don't try to give a speech of introduction strictly from memory. Always make notes. You should also rehearse the introduction until you're confident that you have it down pat. When you arrive at the venue, check with the speaker to see if there are any last-minute changes that need to be made.

Here is an example of an appropriate and effective speech of introduction:

"Good evening, ladies and gentlemen. It's a great pleasure for me to introduce our speaker tonight, who is going to talk to us about the ten most common personal financial planning mistakes. This is a subject in which we should all be deeply interested because it's by avoiding financial mistakes that we can best ensure our financial futures. Our speaker, although having spent almost his entire career advising people on their finances in places like New York, Los Angeles, and Toronto, grew up about thirty miles from where we are right now. He is an award-winning professional accountant who has specialized in personal finances and taxation for over twenty years, and has guided the financial affairs of some of this country's best-known athletes, entertainers, entrepreneurs, and executives. Ladies and gentlemen, please join me in welcoming home Steve Robbins!"

When you arrive at the lectern to perform the actual introduction, remember these ten rules:

1. Stick to meeting the four objectives of a speech of introduction; avoid the temptation to make your own speech, on the topic or anything else.

2. Never try to introduce a speaker from memory; have good notes.

3. Never tell a joke. There are no circumstances that justify telling a joke during a speech of introduction.

4. Keep the introduction as short as possible.

5. Be upbeat and enthusiastic.

6. Avoid clichés such as "a person who needs no introduction" and "without further ado."

7. Look at the audience, not at the speaker, during the introduction; turn toward the speaker only at the very end of the introduction.

8. Start the applause.

9. Wait at the lectern and greet the speaker with a hearty handshake.

10. Go sit down.

Thanking a Speaker

Most "Thank you, Mr./Ms. Speaker" speeches are also dreadful, but they are less harmful than a bad speech of introduction because the main speaker is immune to further damage upon finishing their talk. The most common mistake made by people thanking a speaker is to repeat portions of the speech. This is totally unnecessary, boring at best, and empties the hall at worst.

If you will be thanking the speaker, make a point of introducing yourself to the speaker before the event begins. Tell the speaker you'll be thanking him or her and chat for a moment or two, all the while listening for any points that you might be able to use. Perhaps the speaker had to cut short a trip to keep the engagement. Maybe the speaker came a very great distance to give the talk. If there happens to be anything worthy of note, be sure to mention it. But stay away from clichés such as "taking time out from your busy schedule" or "honoring us with your presence."

Listen intently to the speech and make notes that will help you choose an appropriate adjective or two with which to describe it. You should also note any surprises the speech held, such as an unexpected revelation or a particularly valuable piece of advice.

You can never go wrong by opening your thank-you speech with the simple words: "Thank you very much, Ms. Speaker, for a [insert an appropriate adjective] presentation." Then mention one or two (but no more) worthy points from the speech, such as the revelation or valuable advice. If you did pick up a tidbit about a sacrifice or special effort the speaker had to make to be there, be sure to mention it.

If you're presenting a gift, call the speaker back to the lectern and make the presentation with an appropriate short statement.

If the speaker wishes to say a few words of thanks, that's fine. But never pressure the speaker to do so. If you're also the master of ceremonies, you should then get on with the program. If the events are finished, state that fact, make any closing announcements, thank the people for coming, and move away from the lectern. If you're not the master of ceremonies, just go sit down.

Here's an example of an appropriate and effective thank-you speech:

> "Thank you, Ms. McPherson, for an enlightening and entertaining presentation on the right way to apply for a bank loan; we appreciate having this mysterious area clarified. Your advice to always present an annual budget document to the loan officer showing how we intend to use the loan proceeds and how we'll be able to service the loan is especially useful. The audience may not know this, Ms. McPherson, but we owe you a special vote of thanks for being here because I happened to find out that you delayed your annual golf trip by a couple of days so that you could make it. We really appreciate that. I have a small token of our appreciation here for you, Ms. McPherson. Please accept it with our sincere thanks."

In a nutshell . . .

INTRODUCING A SPEAKER:

1. Get in touch with the speaker and agree on the content of your introduction.
2. Stick to the four objectives of a speech of introduction; the audience didn't come to hear you give a speech or tell jokes.
3. Avoid clichés.

4. Make notes; don't rely on memory.

5. Rehearse.

6. When you arrive at the venue, check with the speaker to see if there are any last-minute changes required.

7. Review the ten rules for when you arrive at the lectern, and stick to them.

THANKING A SPEAKER:

1. Introduce yourself to the speaker and chat for a minute or two. Make note of anything of interest you learn that might be included in your remarks, such as the speaker's having had to make some particular sacrifice to be there.

2. Remember that your job is not to repeat portions of the talk; the audience has already heard it.

3. Listen intently to the speech and make notes that will help you choose an appropriate adjective or two with which to describe it.

4. Make note of any surprises the speech held, such as an unexpected revelation or a particularly valuable piece of advice.

5. Avoid clichés.

ACTING AS A MASTER OF CEREMONIES

When asked to act as a master of ceremonies, you should immediately get all the information outlined in chapter 3, What, Where, When, and to Whom, in respect to the event and its location. Then work closely with the organizers to develop the program and gather the information you will need to fulfill your obligations. This will include:

1. Details of any announcements you will be making

2. The names of all the people you will be introducing, their titles, their roles in the event, and any other information about them that the organizers want you to mention

3. Details of the timing of everything on the schedule, including breaks

4. The names of the technical support people at the venue and how to get in touch with them

5. The name of the senior person from the sponsoring organization who will be present at the event.

You should never act as a master of ceremonies using only notes; you need to prepare a detailed script. Masters of ceremonies often have to contend with last-minute changes, so be sure that the format of your script leaves room for noting any necessary revisions.

Be sure you know the correct pronunciation of all the names you'll be using. It's a good idea to note the phonetic spelling of any unfamiliar or particularly difficult ones.

As in the case of any other public speaking assignment, the only way to find out how your comments as a master of ceremonies will sound is to rehearse them out loud. The more often you rehearse, the more comfortable you're going to be when the actual event rolls around.

Get to the venue well before the scheduled starting time and do a walk-around to be sure that everything that's needed is there and in working order. If anything is amiss, inform the people who can get the problem solved and monitor their progress.

Be sure that everyone who is scheduled to participate in the program is actually present. Introduce yourself to any participants you haven't met before. You should also chat for a moment or two with all participants in order to see if any last-minute changes are required. Remind the speakers of their time limits and how you intend to enforce them. You should also check with the organizers to see whether they have any last-minute changes.

Start on time and do your utmost to keep on schedule. Some organizers don't mind starting late and are soft on speakers who run overtime. Do your best to convince the organizers that it's in everybody's interest to stay on schedule, especially the audience's. But you aren't the boss, so if you're forced to bend things a bit, do so with grace and good humor; nobody benefits from the performance of an obviously disgruntled master of ceremonies.

Don't start the program until you have the full attention of most of the audience, though sometimes you have to actually start talking to get everyone's attention. If you have to take some tough measures to silence the room, be sure to do so good-naturedly. Once the event begins you're in charge, so take charge.

Introduce yourself with a clear, confident voice and indicate your relationship to the event. If you're simply the master of ceremonies, that's all you need to say; if you're also the vice president of marketing of the sponsoring organization, you should make that known right away.

Your job is not to make speeches, but to keep the event moving as scheduled, which means sticking to the script and resisting the temptation to tell jokes or make editorial comments. However, if a short, completely relevant, and worthwhile comment comes into your mind, by all means use it. Under no circumstances, though, should you be seen as trying to upstage any of the participants.

You have a responsibility to both the audience and the organizers to be confident, upbeat, and enthusiastic at all times. If the event is running into difficulty, as the catalyst and tone setter it is even more important for you to maintain a positive tone.

Weddings

Being the master of ceremonies at a wedding reception is different in a number of important respects from other functions. For one thing, you may have to act as the event manager as well as the master of ceremonies. In addition to the general responsibilities outlined above for masters of ceremonies, this will entail:

1. Making sure all the necessary equipment (such as lighting, sound system, lectern, slide show) is available and working

2. Getting people into the room and seated; you should deputize some people to help with this

3. Making some personal comments relevant to the bride and groom and the event; have some ready, but talk briefly and be sure you don't preempt any comments other participants may be making

4. Reminding all the speakers when they'll be speaking and what their time limits are, and checking the tenor of their comments. It's not unusual to have to bolster the confidence of some of the participants and dampen down the enthusiasm (and sometimes the content) of others

5. Being prepared to diplomatically deal with any speakers who have had too much to drink or are rambling on too long, or who start making inappropriate comments

6. Reminding people to sign the guest book and telling them where it is

7. If there are disposable cameras at the tables, reminding the guests to use them and what to do with them when they're finished

8. Appropriately balancing the participation of the two families

9. Making sure you have any congratulatory emails, telegrams, or other messages that you're to read aloud

10. Getting the names (including the correct pronunciation) and hometowns of all out-of-town guests and then recognizing these guests during the event

11. Checking in with the bride and groom about all scheduling requirements, including the cutting of the cake. (You might also want to make sure the cake is there.)

12. Finding out if the parents of the bride and groom are going to join them on the dance floor after the traditional first dance. If so, making sure the parents are aware of their participation.

13. Checking with the bride and groom to see how they want to handle the "tinkling of glasses" ritual and then explaining the rules to the guests

14. Announcing when the formal portion of the event is over and what the rules are for the rest of the evening.

Undoubtedly your two most important objectives as master of ceremonies at a wedding are to make sure everything runs smoothly and do everything in your power to ensure that the bride, the groom, and their guests have a good time.

In a nutshell . . .

1. Work closely with the organizers to develop the program and gather the information you'll need to fulfill your obligations.

2. Prepare a detailed script and be sure the format leaves room for last-minute changes.

3. Be sure you know the correct pronunciation of all names you'll be using.

4. Rehearse.

5. Get to the venue early and ensure that everything that's needed is available and working.

6. Be sure that everyone who is scheduled to participate in the program is there.

7. Briefly go over the program with each participant.

8. Do your utmost to start on time and stay on schedule.

9. Don't start until you have the audience's attention.

10. Introduce yourself in a clear, confident voice and indicate your relationship to the event.

11. You're in charge, so take charge.

12. Remain confident, upbeat, positive, and enthusiastic at all times.

13. Being a master of ceremonies at a wedding entails additional responsibilities, which are outlined in detail in this chapter; familiarize yourself with them.

PRESENTING AND ACCEPTING AN AWARD

Because the presentation of an award requires the same discipline as the introduction of a speaker, you might want to reread that part of chapter 12 as well as this chapter.

Presenting an Award

When presenting an award, you have to remember that you are not the main feature on the program. Keep your remarks to a minimum: no jokes, no editorializing, stick to your script or notes (and you should always use a script or notes).

Following is a foolproof set of rules for presenting an award:

1. If you haven't already been introduced, tell the audience who you are and why you are there.

2. Give a brief history of the award.

3. Outline the criteria that have to be met in order to receive the award.

4. Briefly outline how the recipient met the criteria, being careful to avoid exaggeration.

5. Even if the audience already knows who the winner is, don't mention the recipient's name until the very end, and pause for a beat or two before announcing it with lots of excitement in your voice.

6. Enthusiastically start the applause.

7. If the recipient doesn't know what to do after his or her name is announced, issue a clear invitation to join you at the lectern.

All of this should be carried off in a sincere, businesslike manner with no smart-aleck remarks.

Here is an example of a perfectly appropriate award presentation speech:

"Good evening, ladies and gentlemen. My name is Wendy Russell and it's my honor, as chair of the selection committee, to present this year's Harry Carmichael Memorial Award. The Harry Carmichael Memorial Award was inaugurated in 1985 in memory of the late Harry Carmichael, who was an outstanding athlete and citizen of our city. The recipient of the Harry Carmichael Award must have demonstrated, over a significant period of time, dedication to the promotion of athletics in our city, combined with a strong sense of civic and family duty. It's been said of this year's winner that he puts his whole heart and soul into his community, his sports, and his family. He's a past president of the Kiwanis club. He's a member of the city council. In his younger days he played baseball and football at the high school, college, and state levels. He's coached kids' football and baseball for the past twenty years. He and his wife have raised four outstanding children. Ladies and gentlemen, please acknowledge this year's Harry Carmichael Memorial Award winner . . . Mr. Hank Dalton!"

If Hank remains frozen in his chair, you should say something like, "Okay, Hank, come on up here and receive this honor that you so richly deserve!" When Hank arrives at the lectern, congratulate him, give him his award, and ask him if he'd like to say a few words. When you're finished, go sit down.

Accepting an Award

If you've ever watched an award show, you are aware that acceptance speeches represent another wonderful opportunity to make a bad impression on an audience. This needn't be the case at all. A little thought beforehand, some preparation, and some rehearsal will ensure success.

Before the event, decide whom you will thank and where you will display the award. Be absolutely ruthless when deciding whom to thank, including only those who played a truly important role in your achievement. If you include people who were only marginally involved, you diminish the importance of those whom you could not have done without.

Just as with any other speech, you need to write out and rehearse your acceptance speech in order to have the appropriate form and length. With the exception of the people's names you're going to thank, you probably don't need to have any notes at the lectern, but if you'd be more comfortable having a script or notes, by all means do so. You should definitely write out the names of those you're going to thank, even if there are only two.

You should rehearse your acceptance speech out loud at least two or three times and continue to go over it in your mind whenever you get a chance. Anytime you're attending an event where there is even the remotest chance that you might receive an honor, have something prepared, at least in your mind.

Here is a can't-fail formula for an effective acceptance speech:

1. Thank the sponsoring organization for whatever it is you're receiving (certificate, gift, trophy, plaque, and so on) and acknowledge how you feel about it.

2. If the audience doesn't know what the award is, tell them. For example, you might want to read the citation on a certificate.

3. Briefly thank anyone who played an important role in your achievement.

4. Tell the audience what you intend to do with the award or gift, such as, "This will occupy a place of honor on the fireplace in my den."

5. Close with another simple, general thank you.

Here is an example of an appropriate speech of acceptance:

"I sincerely thank the *Financial Times* for nominating me, and the Press Club for honoring me with this National Business Writing Award. Believe me, ladies and gentlemen, it is a very proud recipient who is standing here before you. I especially want to thank my writing mentor, Dave Scott, whose gentle wisdom and great wit have been instrumental in encouraging me and improving my writing. I also thank my partners who, without complaint, have allowed me the time to indulge in what, for an international accounting firm, is truly a sideline. This certificate will always have a place of honor on my wall. Thank you again."

In a nutshell . . .

PRESENTING AN AWARD:

1. Review the rules for introducing a speaker in chapter 12.
2. Remember that you are not the main feature of the program.
3. Keep your remarks on point and to a minimum.
4. Avoid jokes or editorial comments.
5. Have a script or notes, and stick to them.
6. Follow the format outlined in this chapter.

ACCEPTING AN AWARD:

1. Decide whom you will thank, but include only those who played a truly important role.
2. Decide what you intend to do with the award.
3. Write out your speech.
4. Stick to the formula outlined in this chapter.
5. Rehearse your speech.
6. Keep it short.

DELIVERING A EULOGY

Because funerals and memorial services can be very emotional events, almost everyone gets nervous about delivering eulogies. But there's absolutely no need to worry. Speaking from the heart and keeping your remarks the right length is really all you need to do.

In chapter 1, The Right Topic, I stated that if you feel strongly about a subject, know it well, and really want to talk about it, you couldn't make a poor presentation even if you wanted to. A eulogy for a friend or relative meets all three criteria; therefore you will always do well.

But just because the odds are overwhelmingly in favor of your being successful doesn't mean that there aren't some steps you can take to bolster your confidence and further ensure your success.

If you speak from your heart you will in all probability do just fine speaking "off the cuff." However, it's still a good idea to write out your comments, if not in full then at least in note form. Doing this will:

1. Help you ensure that you've captured all the points you want to make

2. Facilitate the logical organization of your comments; perhaps chronologically, or possibly using anecdotes from various aspects of the life of the deceased, such as family, profession, or hobbies, and so forth

3. Allow you to estimate the length of your remarks; you don't want them to go on longer than necessary.

As in any other speaking situation, you should rehearse. It's not always practical in these circumstances to rehearse out loud at a lectern, but you should at least review your notes a couple of times. If you are particularly nervous, shy, or worried about your performance, go over your remarks in your mind every chance you get until you're comfortable with them.

Even if you write out your speech in full when preparing the eulogy, you should reduce it to note form before standing up to deliver your remarks. If you read from a prepared text your voice will not adequately convey the depth of your feelings, and it's your emotion that the audience can most identify with.

It's not unusual, especially for a family member, to remember something while standing at the lectern that he or she would like to say. It's perfectly in order to ad lib; I actually think it would be a mistake not to mention something that occurs to you at this time—it is obviously meaningful.

In a nutshell . . .

1. Because you meet all the criteria for a successful speaking performance (you feel strongly about the subject; you have earned the right to be up there; and you will want to honor your friend or relative), you will succeed.

2. Writing out your remarks will help you capture all the points you want to cover, make it easier to organize them, and allow you to estimate their length.

3. As in any other speaking situation, don't speak longer than necessary.

4. Rehearse, even if only informally.

5. If you write out your speech in full, reduce it to notes. Reading a speech prevents you from letting your emotions flow through.

6. If an appropriate thought comes to you at the lectern it would probably be a mistake not to mention it.

7. Speak from your heart and keep it relatively short; it really is that simple.

PROPOSING A TOAST

Even if proposing a single toast is the only public speaking that you will ever do, there's still a right and a wrong way to do it. Nevertheless, there is no reason whatsoever why your performance shouldn't be just fine.

As with having to make an impromptu talk (see chapter 11) or deliver a eulogy (see chapter 15), in almost every toasting situation all of the ingredients for a successful talk are present—otherwise you wouldn't have been asked to do it. You will have earned the right to make the toast by virtue of your association with the person being toasted. You will have some emotional investment in the event through your presence at it, which, combined with your respect and fondness for the person being toasted, means you will meet the criterion of feeling strongly about it. Finally, if there's any doubt about the third criterion (wanting to do it), just remind yourself of what an honor it is to be asked and to have the opportunity to express how you feel about the person and the event.

Conversely, if none of the criteria for a successful speaking performance is present—for example if you don't really know the person and have no strong feelings about the event—you should decline the request, even if you're an accomplished public speaker. Everyone, and particularly the guest of honor, will know that you're just playing a role, and your participation will in no way enhance the event; in fact, it's apt to diminish it.

Whether you intend to speak "off the cuff," just use some notes, or speak from a marked-up script, as in every other speaking situation it is extremely useful to initially write out your toast in full (see chapter 5). Writing it out allows you to edit, organize, and time your material as well as to rehearse it. Even a short toast should be rehearsed, if for no other reason than to identify and avoid cumbersome phrasing or words that you have difficulty pronouncing.

And a toast *should* be kept appropriately short and to the point. Furthermore, every statement in it should be both relevant and interesting. Keeping it short, relevant, and interesting will allow you to avoid the most common mistake people fall into when proposing a toast, which is making speeches about themselves. People want to hear about the person being honored, not about you—although it's always appropriate to include information establishing the relationship between you and the person being toasted, provided it's both relevant and interesting. For example, when toasting a bride it might be relevant that you met her through playing bridge with her parents, but it's not too interesting; remarks about her university history thesis might be interesting, but not too relevant (unless, of course, that's how she met you or the groom).

The admonition to never tell a joke in front of an audience is present throughout this book; never is it more important than when proposing a toast. I cannot think of a single toasting situation in which telling a joke would be appropriate. However, it's fine to include an amusing anecdote involving the person being toasted, particularly if it's combined with establishing your personal relationship.

The length of a toast depends entirely on the nature of the event and your relationship with the person being toasted. If your toast is only one of many throughout an evening during which a number of different people are being honored, you should keep it very short—not more than a minute or so. On the other hand, when toasting the bride or groom, it's perfectly acceptable to speak for up to five minutes or more, provided always that your remarks are both relevant and interesting.

Avoid the temptation to look at the person you're toasting until the very end of your toast. Instead, make eye contact with all parts of the audience until you ask them to join you in the toast. Then raise your glass, turn to the person being toasted, and conclude your remarks, emphatically and clearly, with the actual "To the bride!" or "To Sam!"

In a nutshell . . .

1. Even if a single toast is the only public speaking you ever do, there's still a right and a wrong way to do it.

2. All of the criteria for a successful public-speaking performance are usually met in a toasting situation; that is, you know the person, care about the event, and recognize the honor of being asked to propose a toast.

3. If none of the criteria is present, you should decline the request.

4. Writing out your toast in full will allow you to edit, organize, and time it.

5. Even a short toast needs to be rehearsed.

6. Every remark made in a toast should be *both* relevant and interesting.

7. Keeping a toast short and to the point will allow you to avoid making a speech about yourself.

8. It's always appropriate, and usually desirable, to include information establishing the relationship between you and the person being toasted, provided it's both relevant and interesting.

9. Never tell a joke; but it's fine to include an amusing anecdote involving the person being toasted, particularly if it's combined with establishing your personal relationship.

10. The length of your toast depends entirely on the circumstances of the event and your relationship with the person being toasted.

11. Make your remarks to the audience, not to the person who is being toasted; turn to the person being toasted only after inviting the audience to join you in raising their glasses.

12. Make the actual toast directly to the guest of honor, speaking emphatically and clearly.

Chapter

17

CHAIRING A MEETING

Because chairing a meeting entails constantly addressing a group of people, albeit for short periods at a time, the skills and techniques discussed in this book apply. People who have established their credentials as effective speakers and leaders are frequently asked to chair meetings.

To run efficient meetings, and thereby enhance your reputation as a leader, you should consistently apply the following rules:

1. Although you never want to be seen as an officious and inflexible leader, it's a good idea to have an appreciation of some of the fundamental rules of parliamentary procedure, such as the procedures for dealing with formal motions or motions from the floor, the correct procedures for taking notes, decorum in debate, and closing debates.

2. Control the seating. Arrange for people who tend to argue with each other to sit on the same side of the table. Confrontations will be fewer and shorter if they aren't facing each other.

3. Start on time, even if there is only one other person there. It won't take long for the message to get through and the number of latecomers will diminish with each meeting.

4. Open with a brief statement of what you expect to accomplish, announce the time of adjournment, and stick to it.

5. Ask if anyone is expecting any emergency messages on their cell phones, pagers, or PDAs. Ask those who aren't expecting critical messages to turn off their devices.

6. Ask if anyone has any new business to add to the agenda. If time is limited, either the new item or an existing agenda item will have to be deferred. Make and announce this decision right away.

7. Be confident and enthusiastic, but remember that it's your responsibility to keep the meeting moving, on schedule and on topic.

8. Watch your tone of voice and body language; you always want to convey an image of leadership and of being in control.

9. Keep breaks to a minimum, but never go more than two hours without at least a leg stretch.

10. Listen intently to all speakers.

11. Don't introduce your own thoughts on an agenda item until it's obvious no one else is going to raise your points.

12. Encourage everyone to participate, but never embarrass or force anyone into speaking.

13. Don't let anyone dominate the discussion.

14. Make brief notes of key points; don't rely on the secretary's minutes being as complete as you'd like them to be.

15. Finish on time.

In a nutshell . . .

1. Effectively chairing a meeting entails many of the skills and techniques discussed in this book.

2. Once you've established your credentials as an effective speaker, you're more apt to be asked to chair meetings. Effectively chairing meetings will in turn reinforce your reputation as a leader.

3. Until they become second nature to you, never chair a meeting without reviewing the rules set forth in this chapter.

Chapter 18

BECOMING A MORE INTERESTING SPEAKER

No matter how experienced and comfortable you become in front of groups, there is always room to become an even more interesting speaker. Broadening your horizons and interests will enhance the knowledge and skills you already possess and help you acquire new, beneficial ones. And of course you need to approach everything you do with the right attitude.

Knowledge

There are three ways to acquire knowledge: study, experience, and being around people who know more than you do. All three methods are useful, but the most efficient is study. Reading is to the mind what exercise is to the body. Those who don't read are no better off than those who can't read.

A sure way to become a boring person, and by extension a boring speaker, is to be interested only in your work. To be a better-informed and more interesting person and speaker, at least one-quarter of your reading should be outside your occupational field. This will help you enormously in developing appropriate analogies and illustrations for your talks.

Experience is a wonderful teacher, and yours will provide you with a store of examples that you can use as evidence in your speeches. Try to learn from everything that happens around you. Make notes of interesting observations, opinions, quotations, and statistics, and develop a filing system that will allow you to easily find and refer to this material when you're preparing a talk.

Never put a limit on your search for knowledge. There's no such thing as an uninteresting subject, just uninterested people. Until you understand something completely, be open-minded about it; become interested before you become judgmental. The person who knows how something is done can give a good speech about it, but the person who knows why it is done will give a great speech.

Two areas of knowledge that you should never stop developing are your vocabulary and your grasp of grammar. Being able to find the precise words and use them correctly will help enormously in speech preparation and delivery. Anytime you encounter a word that you don't know the meaning or pronunciation of, look it up in a dictionary and make it a part of your vocabulary. You should also take note of the synonyms and antonyms listed for such words. Doing crossword puzzles is a fun way to improve your vocabulary.

Skills

You must continually hone the skills you have through use, while at the same time acquiring new skills that will enhance your speaking ability. Possessing a single talent will take you only so far, and will definitely limit your scope as a speaker. There are three good ways to identify the skills you already possess and to discover those that may be lacking.

Most people don't have a problem with the first method—it's simply objectively assessing what you do and don't do well. However, it's sometimes difficult to be sufficiently objective, so the second method is to ask others, such as colleagues, bosses, and mentors, for their assessments. Finally, and this is the method most often overlooked, you have to try new things and try doing old things in new ways.

Putting a limit on what you will do puts a limit on what you can do. If you try new things or doing old things in new ways, you might discover a skill that you didn't know you had and you might identify a skill that you should or would like to develop. Opportunities are never missed; other people will take advantage of those you don't. When you aren't improving, someone else is, and when you encounter that person, you will come in second.

The skills you need to acquire are often evident in your surroundings. Always ask yourself which skills would help you enhance the application of your knowledge, whatever you're going to be doing, wherever you're going to be doing it. For example, the engineer who designs a product and then decides to sell it should take some sales training. It's usually instructive to ask successful people in your field to recommend areas for improvement.

Attitude

Not only do you need to develop positive attitudes about yourself, but you must also understand the attitudes of people you deal with, especially those of your audience members. An audience is not an amorphous mass; it's made up of individuals who react as individuals.

However, we're all similar when it comes to how we want to be treated. We want to be liked and we want to feel important. To become a more interesting person and speaker, you need to treat people as if you like them and find ways to sincerely make them feel important. There is nothing hypocritical about this. Everyone, by virtue of being human, has the right to be treated decently; if you can't find some way to make a person feel important, at least never make them feel unimportant.

When you develop the right attitude toward other people, you will carry it over in your role as a speaker and you will understand, and relate to, your audiences more effectively. Audiences have a keen sense of how you feel about them.

Many years ago there was a *Ripley's Believe It or Not* cartoon depicting an ordinary iron bar worth about $5. The cartoon then pointed out that the iron bar made into horseshoes would be worth about $10. Made into sewing needles, it would be worth $3,285. If it was turned into balance springs for watches, it would be worth $250,000, an increase of 50,000 percent! Knowledge and skills are very much like that iron bar. They're worth only what you do with them.

In a nutshell . . .

1. Continually expand your skills and knowledge base, particularly your vocabulary and grammar.

2. At least one-quarter of your reading should be outside your field of work, which will help you develop appropriate analogies, examples, and illustrations for your talks.

3. Be observant; try to learn from everything that goes on around you.

4. Make extensive notes.

5. Develop a filing system that will allow you to easily find and refer to your notes.

6. There's no such thing as an uninteresting subject, just uninterested people.

7. Be open-minded; become interested before you become judgmental.

8. Try doing new things and doing old things in new ways.

9. Learn how to understand people.

10. Remember that an audience is not an amorphous mass; it's made up of individuals who react as individuals.

11. Always consider your audience's point of view.

12. Your knowledge and skills are worth only what you do with them.

Chapter 19

DON'T WRECK YOUR CAREER AT THE LECTERN

As mentioned in chapter 2, Managing Fear, although one or two poor performances are not likely to irrevocably tarnish your reputation, especially in the early stages of your public speaking activity, consistently subpar speaking efforts can wreck a career. I've seen it happen.

Many times throughout my professional life I've seen knowledgeable, otherwise skilled people lose out on opportunities and promotions simply because they could not communicate their messages effectively in front of groups. The reason for not promoting or hiring a person is often that person's apparent lack of ability to positively influence others. You don't hear this said about people who have developed into influential speakers.

On one memorable occasion, I was in a large audience to hear a then-well-known economist give a talk based on her recently published book. It was a dreadful performance. All the chatter on the way out was about what a surprisingly poor speaker she was, rather than about the merits of her ideas. Only three or four people bought her book; since selling books was probably the main purpose of the event, her evening was a failure in every respect. If she strung together a series of such performances, people would probably stop buying her books altogether. Maybe they did. She certainly hasn't been a fixture on the speaking circuit for some time and hasn't written any books lately.

Although poor speaking performances can damage your reputation, don't get downhearted; there is good news. The other side of the coin is that consistently good performances can be just the ingredient to launch and sustain a very successful career. Whatever your field may be, good speaking performances will enhance your reputation, sometimes beyond your wildest expectations.

There's even more good news. Anyone can become an accomplished public speaker. You need to be knowledgeable about your subject and you need to care about your subject. That part is easy; you probably have, right now, more than one topic that fits the bill. However, acquiring the skills and developing the techniques that separate the memorable speakers from the forgettable speakers does require some hard work and practice. Everything you need to know about those skills and techniques is in this book, and none of it is beyond your ability to accomplish.

One of the first statements you read in this book is worth repeating as the last: communicate well and do well; communicate best and flourish.

In a nutshell . . .

1. Consistently subpar speaking performances can wreck a career and seriously damage a reputation.

2. Consistently good speaking performances can enormously enhance a career and a reputation.

3. Public speaking skills can be learned.

4. Always refer to this book when you have a presentation to make.

Index

A

Acceptance speeches, 122–23, 124
Active voice, 44
After-dinner presentations, 30
Alliteration, 40
Analogies, 47–48
Appearance, 87
Armstrong, Neil, 53
Attitude
  of audience, 138
  developing right, 13–14, 138
Audience
  antagonistic, 32
  attitude of, 138
  changes in expected, 74
  changing script and

  delivery for, 95
  circulating among, before speech, 74
  complimenting, 53–54
  concern for, 17, 31–33
  expectations of, 14–15, 22–23, 32
  hecklers in, 81–82
  identifying with, 54, 55
  importance of opening to, 53–54
  knowledgeable people in, 8, 14
  learning about, 22–23
  participation, 81–82
  questions from, 92–98
  relevance of evidence for, 48
  size of, 23

MORE REFERENCE, CAREER, AND BUSINESS BOOKS FROM TEN SPEED PRESS

Write Right!
A Desktop Digest of Punctuation, Grammar, and Style
4TH EDITION
JAN VENOLIA

"An invaluable tool for executives, secretaries, students… it illustrates the right and wrong way by easy-to-grasp examples."

—Los Angeles Times

5³⁄₈ x 7 inches, 224 pages
$12.95 paper (Can $17.95)
ISBN-13: 978-1-58008-328-7

Rewrite Right!
Your Guide to Perfectly Polished Prose
2ND EDITION
JAN VENOLIA

This definitive guide will help writers of all levels improve the quality of their work and harness the power of language.

5³⁄₈ x 7 inches, 200 pages
$12.95 paper (Can $17.95)
ISBN-13: 978-1-58008-239-6

continued →

MORE REFERENCE, CAREER, AND BUSINESS BOOKS FROM TEN SPEED PRESS

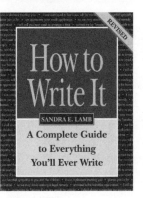

Nitty-Gritty Grammar
A Not-So-Serious Guide to Clear Communication
EDITH FINE AND JUDITH P. JOSEPHSON

A lively, user-friendly guide to effective communication, designed for people who want to refresh, review, or polish their skills. *Nitty-Gritty Grammar* makes learning the rules of English fun.

6 x 9 inches, 112 pages
$9.95 paper (Can $13.95)
ISBN-13: 978-0-89815-966-0

How to Write It
A Complete Guide to Everything You'll Ever Write
REVISED EDITION
SANDRA E. LAMB

A time-saving compendium of over 250 samples of every type of letter and document, from the ones we enjoy writing to the ones we dread.

8 1/2 x 11 inches, 352 pages
$19.95 paper (Can $25.95)
ISBN-13: 978-1-58008-572-4

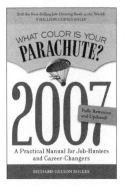

MORE REFERENCE, CAREER, AND BUSINESS BOOKS FROM TEN SPEED PRESS

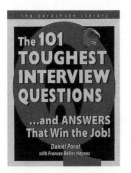

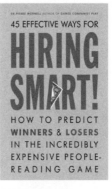

The 101 Toughest Interview Questions
...and Answers that Win the Job!
DANIEL POROT

A concise and effective approach to calming your nerves and facing even the most stressful interview situation with confidence and poise.

4 1/8 x 5 1/4 inches, 240 pages
$12.95 paper (Can $17.95)
ISBN-13: 978-1-58008-068-2

Hiring Smart!
How to Predict Winners & Losers in the Incredibly Expensive People-Reading Game
PIERRE MORNELL

Dr. Pierre Mornell distills fifteen years of experience in the hiring front lines to present forty-five strategies designed to take the measure of a candidate, emphasizing behavior, not words.

7 x 10 inches, 240 pages, full color
$19.95 paper (Can $29.95)
ISBN-13: 978-1-58008-514-4